T0088092

LIVING TRUSTS *for Everyone*

LIVING TRUSTS *for Everyone*

SECOND EDITION

Why a Will Is Not the Way to Avoid Probate, Protect Heirs, and Settle Estates

RONALD FARRINGTON SHARP

ALLWORTH PRESS

Copyright © 2017 by Ronald Farrington Sharp

All Rights Reserved. Copyright under Berne Copyright Convention, Universal Copyright Convention, and Pan American Copyright Convention. No part of this book may be reproduced, stored in a retrieval system, or transmitted in any form, or by any means, electronic, mechanical, photocopying, recording or otherwise, without the express written consent of the publisher, except in the case of brief excerpts in critical reviews or articles. All inquiries should be addressed to Allworth Press, 307 West 36th Street, 11th Floor, New York, NY 10018.

Allworth Press books may be purchased in bulk at special discounts for sales promotion, corporate gifts, fund-raising, or educational purposes. Special editions can also be created to specifications. For details, contact the Special Sales Department, Allworth Press, 307 West 36th Street, 11th Floor, New York, NY 10018 or info@skyhorsepublishing.com.

25 24 23 11 10 9

Published by Allworth Press, an imprint of Skyhorse Publishing, Inc. 307 West 36th Street, 11th Floor, New York, NY 10018.

Allworth Press® is a registered trademark of Skyhorse Publishing, Inc.®, a Delaware corporation.

www.allworth.com

Cover design by Esther Wu and Mary Belibasakis

Print ISBN: 978-1-62153-567-6
Ebook ISBN: 978-1-62153-570-6

Printed in the United States of America

This book is not intended as legal or tax advice as laws vary from jurisdiction to jurisdiction and change frequently. If you have legal questions about your particular situation, you should consult an attorney in your state.

Contents

Preface to the Second Edition vii
Introduction xiii
Chapter One:
Trusts and Wills Defined 1
Chapter Two:
You Must Have a Trust If . . . 11
Chapter Three:
A Comparison: Trusts and Wills 25
Chapter Four:
Trust Seminars: A Free Meal, But at What Cost? 33
Chapter Five:
Watch Out for Attorneys 39
Chapter Six:
Trustees 53
Chapter Seven:
Making Your Trust Work: Funding 61
Chapter Eight:
Instructions to You as the Grantor and Trustee 69
Chapter Nine:
You Do Not Need a Trust If . . . 73
Chapter Ten:
The Many Types of Trusts 79
Chapter Eleven:
Problems with Trusts 85
Chapter Twelve:
Guardians, Powers of Attorney, and Other Documents 91
Chapter Thirteen:
Trustee Instructions for Death or Disability of the Trust Owner 101
Appendix A:
Forms and Form Letters 127

Appendix B:
Short Form: Guide to Trust Funding 143
Appendix C:
Decision-Making for Your Estate Plan Form 147
Appendix D:
Asset Listing Form 155
Appendix E:
FAQs 157

Glossary of Terms 165
Index 169

Preface to the Second Edition

A second edition of *Living Trusts for Everyone* seemed timely given significant changes in the law. I have updated, rewritten, and expanded sections in response to reader feedback. The first edition was very well received, and I have gotten numerous emails thanking me for making this information available. I have rewritten much of the text just for my own purposes to make it more readable, so I hope you find this new edition educational and useful.

You will now find information on the federal estate tax that may enable you to simplify an existing trust or allow you to create a new one with fewer complications. The trust you create now should be easier to understand and should be less expensive to set up due to simple trusts now being appropriate for nearly everyone.

Nowadays, there are many more kinds of assets to protect than there were even a few years ago. Such things as online investment accounts, banking, credit cards, websites, domain names, and even online gaming or gambling accounts as well as other intangible assets often have significant value and need to be brought under the umbrella of trust protection.

Former clients and readers of the book have reported real concerns with trustees who ignore the trust instructions, fail to communicate with the heirs of an estate, waste or even steal the estate assets, and commit other malfeasance. I go over ways to set up your trust so that these sorts of actions are eliminated or minimized.

More information is included on how to deal with trust assets during your lifetime. For example, how does the trust sell real estate? What are trust certificates, and why do banks and title companies want new ones all the time? When and how can a trust be cancelled? When should a trust be made irrevocable? How about incapacity—should you define the specifics as to what constitutes mental incapacity and who makes that decision? A new FAQ section covers common concerns with specific examples.

While I do not recommend doing your own trust or using a fill-in-the-blank form, I have set out the decisions you need to make before you ever visit a lawyer so that you have had time to discuss and think about your options. Who gets what and when are some of the decisions, but who is in charge and under what circumstances are others. Having these decisions made ahead of time should reduce the attorney time and—we hope —your attorney fees.

I have seen attorneys actually giving away free copies of *Living Trusts for Everyone* as an assist to their clients in understanding the basics of trusts, so I know the book has been well used.

Much has been written about using the living trust to avoid probate. One would assume from the information out there that probate avoidance is the most important value of having a trust. But, for many people, there are far more important and even critical reasons to have a trust rather than a will.

There are four fundamental purposes and advantages of a trust.

The first is asset management. It could be a mistake to give certain beneficiaries a lump sum inheritance. They may be too young to properly manage money on their own, may be mentally incapable of managing it, or may not have enough maturity or good sense to be good money managers. Using a will to leave your assets to your young children may result in money going to someone too young to properly manage it. Trusts solve that problem.

Minors can inherit from their parents or others. Unless the inheritance is left to them in a trust, the money would be kept for them by their guardian and conservator. Then, when they reach the "age of majority" (adulthood—usually eighteen), whatever is left of the money they inherit is turned over to them as a lump sum whether they are responsible with money or not.

Even adult heirs may be incapable of managing money properly. Having their share in trust for them allows someone else to be sure it is properly invested and managed. Those who receive certain governmental benefits, including disabled heirs who need help with medical costs and rely on Medicaid, may be disqualified from receiving those benefits if they inherit too much that is not in the right sort of trust for them.

The second benefit is tax reduction. While the estate tax now hits fewer people than before due to the high threshold, a trust of one kind or another can either eliminate or greatly reduce estate and inheritance taxes. This purpose is considered by many nonexpert attorneys to be the only reason to have a trust—thus their oft-given yet erroneous advice: you don't have enough money to need a trust.

The third advantage is probate avoidance, which is a valuable benefit. The big lie put forth by some attorneys and bar associations is that probate is not that expensive and there is no good reason to try to avoid it. The truth is that probate is usually very expensive (because of attorney fees) and is in nearly all cases totally unnecessary if a properly prepared and funded living trust had been prepared. Attorneys who say a trust is not needed are either unaware of the value of trusts or have a vested interest in seeing probate continue.

The fourth benefit is for those who wish to avoid a court-ordered conservatorship should they become so disabled as to be unable to manage their own affairs. If, for example, a person has dementia, the trust can have provisions that allow a successor trustee (the one who would take control at death or disability) to take over financial management of the trust assets. This helps the person avoid the expense and embarrassment of court supervision.

There is also a grab bag of additional benefits, including privacy (probate is public record; trusts are most often not), low cost (there are no court costs, filing fees, or estate inventory fees on a trust at death), ease of administration, lower likelihood of someone contesting the estate, and elimination of the time delay caused by probate of a will.

I have also included in this volume a set of instructions for the family to follow at the death or disability of the trust maker. Most often, attorneys do not provide instructions and the family has no idea what to do when the trust maker dies. So they go back to the attorney who prepared the trust and end up paying a lot of money to find out what to do. The fact is that a trustee does not need legal services to settle the trust because the things that need to be done are mostly clerical, not legal, in nature. Why pay attorney rates for clerical work? The information in this section is invaluable and not available from most sources.

The information contained herein will benefit both those who do not have a trust as well as those who do. This is not a textbook or a comprehensive treatise on all the many kinds of trusts that can be done for various reasons, nor will you find out how to do your own trust. This is a book for the 95 percent of the population that has done no estate planning, so that they are informed and will not be misled by incorrect information pushed by those with vested interests in seeing the probate process continue.

Introduction

When I was in law school back in 1973, I took an introductory course on trusts and estates. Our class was visited by an old-time lawyer (probably about the age I am right now) who gave us what he considered practical and useful advice in starting out in the practice of law. I will paraphrase his advice as I remember it.

We were in one of the big lecture halls and he stood onstage at the podium, then began to pace much as I imagined he did while talking to a jury.

When you young people get done with law school and pass the bar, most of you will be going into private practice. You will meet a lot of people who want you to do their wills. A lot of them will be your own age. I am going to tell you how to make the most of this opportunity.

Now, you don't make much money on a will. In fact, you don't want to. Consider it a loss leader. The thing to do is do these wills real cheap. Word will get out and you will have a lot of wills to do. How you do it is important. First, when you write it up, be sure to put in that they want you to be the attorney who handles the estate—put it right in the will. Get some nice printed-up will paperwork with fancy lettering and your name and address printed on the envelope. Then, make sure that you have a Will File. Keep the original copy of the will and give the client a photocopy and a receipt for the original. Tell them this is normal procedure so the will is kept safe.

Now what will happen is that as the years go by your Will File gets bigger and bigger. Then, your clients start to die off. When they do, the family has to come to you because you have the will. Naturally, they expect that you will be the lawyer for the estate, since you are named in the will and have the original. So now, as you reach the last half of your practice, you have a built-in probate practice. Probate is very lucrative. This, ladies and gentlemen, is your retirement plan.

I thought then (and still do) that this was a very sleazy tactic—one that gives all lawyers a bad name. We have enough trouble with our public image as it is. Yet this practice is still going on and no one is the wiser. Clients are not getting the proper advice and planning they rely on, and lawyers are profiting.

The fact is that in most cases, probate is not necessary and is easily avoided. If proper planning is done, there should be no legal fees at all after a person's death other than a possible question-and-answer conference.

I have found that people are lost at sea when a person dies and seek help—usually from a lawyer. They are then charged hundreds of dollars an hour for many hours simply because only the lawyer knows what needs to be done at death, even if the deceased has made very careful plans to simplify the estate and keep it out of probate. So included as the last chapter is an actual set of step-by-step instructions—the secret is now out of what to do at death.

I hope that I have explained trusts in a simple and understandable way so you as the reader and potential client know as much about trusts as most of the lawyers out there.

CHAPTER ONE

Trusts and Wills Defined

Years ago, I started doing revocable trusts as a way of helping my clients avoid the long delays and high costs of probate. Now, after having done nearly four thousand trust-based estate plans, I can confidently assure you that a will is not the way to plan your estate.

Wills have to be probated.

Trusts don't.

Most people believe good estate planning is having a last will and testament made up by their local lawyer. Most people are wrong. The reason they believe wills are good is because the lawyer tells them so. It may be that the lawyer really believes that probate isn't so bad, but there are two other reasons for this advice. First is that many attorneys are not familiar with trusts and so do not recommend them. That is why I received many referrals from other attorneys whose clients wanted a trust and their lawyer didn't know enough about them to prepare one. The other reason frankly is that lawyers have a vested interest in seeing you go through probate. Most of the cost of probate is attorney fees. It is not, as they would have you believe, "court costs."

The actual cost of probate is unpredictable in most cases. It is usually based on the hourly rate of the lawyer—which may be hundreds of dollars per hour—multiplied by the total amount of time to complete the case. There can be a big incentive to "bill hours." Every telephone call, letter, meeting, and court appearance is recorded and billed. Since probate cases usually go on for one, two, or three years, the cost can be very high indeed. And attorney hourly rates vary widely. Hourly rates for probate work may run from $150 to $500 per hour, so it doesn't take long for the bill to get very large.

The family that hires the attorney rarely complains about the fees, thinking that there is nothing that can be done, and accepts whatever is billed to the estate. Here is a tip and something most people do not realize: attorney fees are negotiable in most cases, and you can also, even in a probate case, ask the attorney to allow family members to do as much of the nonlegal work as possible to keep the bill down. This is rarely done, and no one has ever asked me to do this. I typically give my clients homework—things they can do themselves to fund the trust rather than paying me.

Probate is, for the most part, pretty simple stuff. Except in contested cases or where litigation is needed, the probate process consists of filing a series of fill-in-the-blank forms in the right sequence and timeframe. It is not unusual for a legal assistant or secretary to fill out the forms. The attorney involvement in the process is typically very minimal, even though the case is often billed as if the attorney was hands-on every step of the way. The point is that you are paying a lot of money for what amounts to clerical work.

It's not always billable hours. Certain states set the attorney fee portion of the probate cost as a percentage of the gross estate. This may actually be even more unfair than the hourly rate method. In California, for example, the following are the maximum rates that attorneys can charge for probate (and you can bet that nearly everybody is going to charge the maximum).

4 percent on the first $15,000
3 percent on the next $85,000
2 percent on the next $900,000
1 percent on the next $9 million
0.5 percent on the next $15 million

So a typical $500,000 estate would have attorney fees of $13,000—a lot of money. However, the executor (also called the personal representative) would be entitled to an additional $13,000 fee. So now, we are up to $26,000 and have not included the cost of bonds, filing fees, inventory tax, and publication costs. This is, in my opinion, a very unfair way for costs to be assessed. It may take no more effort or time to probate a $150,000 estate than it does a $500,000 one, yet the fees are vastly different and not related to the effort expended or expertise needed. Most states have gotten away from the percentage fee because of this disparity—but an hourly rate may actually end up costing the estate more. Court costs are now being looked at as a source of revenue for the state. Filing fees are typically several hundred dollars. This is in addition, of course, to executor fees and attorney fees. Then there is the tax levied on the size of the probate case in some states. This is sometimes called an "inventory fee" and is a percentage of the total estate paid to the court or the county treasurer. Personally, whenever I write a check to the government, I think of it as a tax by another name. None of these costs are incurred in independent trust administration.

The time involved is another big problem with probate. The probate case may have a minimum time under state law that it must be "open" to allow potential creditors of the deceased to present claims against the estate. Even in a simple one-asset estate, the case may have to stay open for a minimum of six months. But because there are no firm deadlines in probate, many attorneys put off finishing it and concentrate on their cases that do have deadlines, like court trials and real estate closings. The probate estate can be kept on the bottom of the pile. I have read that the average time to close a probate case is fifteen to eighteen months. This will vary from state to state and attorney to attorney, with some estates being kept open for years. Fees continue to accumulate for "file reviews," so why not keep it going?

So avoiding probate is a big deal, no matter what your lawyer tells you. And the living trust is the best way to do it.

According to the National Association of Estate Planning Councils, only about 5 percent of people with an estate have done any estate planning at all. And most of those have done a will rather than a trust. For those who die without a will, most folks rely on state law to determine what happens to their estate at death. A will may be better than nothing at all, but it pales in comparison to the value of a trust.

Before we go too far, let's define our terms. What exactly is the difference between a will and a trust?

WHAT IS A WILL?

A will is really just a written document telling who gets what part of your stuff at your death, when they get it, and who is in charge of getting the assets to the people who are supposed to get them. You can write your own will in your own handwriting (what lawyers call a holographic will) or it can be typed up, usually by a lawyer, and ceremonially witnessed and/or notarized. You can buy a will online or even get a fill-in-the-blank one at the office supply store. Some states even have a state-promulgated "statutory will," which is another fill-in-the-blank form. Wills are pretty easy to make and are usually less expensive to create than a trust. The big cost of a will comes later when the probate fees are counted in.

The executor (also called the personal representative or sometimes the administrator) is the one who is in charge of seeing that these written instructions in the will are carried out under the supervision of the court.

The instructions in the will are really instructions to the probate court—who gets what, when they get it, and who's in charge. After your death, if there is anything left in your name to be probated, it is necessary to file the will in probate court because a court order is the only way your heirs can get your stuff turned over to them legally. You can't just take the will to the bank, show it to them, and walk out with your inheritance. There are a number of ways to avoid having things in your own name that have to be probated, such as giving everything away before you die or having everything in joint ownership, but these methods have problems of their own, which will be explained later in this book.

For example, I had a client who married a woman who owned a house in her name only. They lived in her house together for years, and he even signed on to the mortgage when it was refinanced. She then died suddenly. The house was in her name alone and his name was never added to the deed. Her husband was very upset when I explained that the house was not his until the probate court said so. She had made a will which left everything to him, but that was not in itself enough—which was a big surprise to him. He could not get full title to the house transferred to him until the probate court process was completed and all the expenses were paid. That case cost thousands of dollars in probate costs because of poor planning.

Here's another example: Dad dies, leaving no wife but three adult children. He has a house and some bank accounts and other investments. He has a will that says everything goes equally to his children. In order for those children to sell the house, they need to prove they own it. Unfortunately, in most cases, the will in itself is not sufficient proof for a land title company or a real estate mortgage company that the house now belongs to the children—they want a court order that says the will is valid and that the property belongs to the children. The will has to be probated to get that order and clear the title.

Interestingly, in most states the will in the above example is totally useless and was a waste of money for Dad. The reason is that if a person dies without a will, then state law determines who are a person's heirs. These laws are called the laws of descent and distribution in case of intestacy (who gets what when somebody dies without a will). In the Dad-and-three-kids example, most state laws say that children whose parent dies without a spouse share his estate equally. A will adds nothing to that. The probate process is virtually identical with or without a will, so whoever charged Dad for that will did nothing for the money. Dad should have had a trust.

WHAT IS A TRUST?

A trust is also just a written document. It also says who gets what, when they get it, and who is in charge of seeing that that happens. The person in charge is the trustee. The difference between it and a will is that a trust does not have to go through the probate court.

The reason a trust is not probated is that when a trust is signed, it becomes a legal entity that has the ability to own things. I often analogize it to the hardware store down the street. Smith's Hardware is a corporation. The corporation owns the building, the inventory, the delivery truck, the hardware bank account, the money in the cash register—all the hardware store assets. The Smiths own the corporation. If they die, the corporation is in a sense still alive and will keep selling hardware. New owners come in and take over the business operation.

A trust is similar. In a trust, the trust owners (called variously the grantors, trustors, or settlors) transfer their assets into the name of the trust. Let's call it the Smith Trust. After they sign the trust document, the Smiths then "fund" the trust. In other words, they transfer their assets into the trust name. This is done in a few ways, but typically real estate is deeded into the name of the trust by using a quitclaim deed. Bank accounts may either be put into the name of the Smith Trust or may pay on death (POD) to the trust (kind of like a beneficiary designation). Life insurance is transferred by naming the trust as the beneficiary. Tax-deferred accounts like IRAs and 401(k)s may have the trust as the primary or contingent beneficiary.

The idea is to have the Smith Trust own all the Smiths' assets. That way, at the death of the Smiths, there is nothing left in their individual names for the probate court to administer. The trust owns their stuff, but they own the trust. They die and the trust still owns their stuff, but the trust document instructions then kick in. The trust says who takes over at their death to carry out their instructions as to who gets what and when.

The great thing is that there is no court order needed for the trustee to take over after the Smiths die. The trustee merely has to show proof that they are dead and show the trust to prove who is the trustee. Then, literally the day after they die and without any fees, the trustee can begin carrying out the Smiths' instructions on distributing the trust assets. (How the trustee does all this step by step is explained in simple language later in this book.)

Now, of course, the trustee still has to do the normal things that need to be done when a person dies. The garage has to be cleaned out, the credit card bills and funeral and burial expenses need to be paid, and the last year's income tax must be filed, but the trustee just goes ahead and does these things. No lawyer is needed and no legal or court fees are due.

People worry that a trust will tie up their property or complicate things during their lifetime. Not true. In a revocable trust, the trust owners (grantors) have full rights to all trust assets during their lifetime. They can sell these, give them away, mortgage them, or even burn them up or gamble them away if they want without anyone's permission or any special paperwork. A trust is a death-planning device and does not complicate the owner's life—if it is put together properly.

After the death or disability of the grantors the named trustee is in charge but does not have the same powers that the trust grantor had. We call a trustee that name because this is someone the grantor picks who is trustworthy. Trustees have legal responsibilities to the trust beneficiaries. Trustees cannot, in most cases, change the terms of the trust in the way the grantors can. They can only follow the instructions of the grantors. And the trustee cannot do anything risky with the trust assets. State law requires a trustee to be very conservative in investing and dealing with trust assets. A trustee is called a "fiduciary" because they have a special responsibility to the beneficiaries to safeguard the trust assets for the benefit of the beneficiaries until all the trust assets are ultimately distributed as the grantors have instructed.

Bottom line? It is infinitely faster and cheaper to settle an estate with a trust rather than with a court-supervised probate of a will.

Your own lawyer may tell you that a simple will is all you need and that you do not have enough assets to consider a trust. Your lawyer is either lying to you or is uninformed of the facts about trusts. Many lawyers have been minimally trained in trust law and believe that the only reason to have a trust is for wealthy people to avoid estate taxes. Wrong.

The fact is that nearly everyone would be better off with a trust than with a will. In most cases, the only person who benefits from your having a will instead of a trust is your lawyer. Attorney fees for making the will and probating the estate are an estate lawyer's bread and butter.

Of course, sometimes a lawyer can arrange it so a trust is no better or cheaper than a will. Some attorneys charge what they call a "settlement fee" to help the family wrap up the trust after death. This may be a percentage of the trust assets. The services provided by the lawyers are not, for the most part, legal services, but they are charged just as if they were. They may also charge outrageous fees to prepare a trust, or prepare a complex trust when a simple one would work just fine. I will speak more to the issue of attorney fees and trust settlement later.

I have been talking so far about a simple trust for the normal family situation—what the IRS calls a revocable grantor trust and which is often called a living trust. There are a lot of kinds of trusts with a lot of functions, including estate tax avoidance and charitable purposes, but most of the situations normal people find themselves in are easily handled using a simple revocable trust. In the next chapter, I will explain who absolutely should have a trust and what it will do for them.

One more note: it is possible to put the provisions for a trust in the language of the last will and testament. A trust of this kind is called a testamentary trust. It may contain all the provisions of a stand-alone trust document and accomplish the same things. But because it is in a will, the trust is not created until probate is finished. It is then funded with some or all of the assets left after the probate process is completed and all the costs deducted.

Anyone with this type of trust is losing the major benefit of probate avoidance. This is not the type of trust you want. The testamentary trust is a great deal for the lawyer, because he gets paid for preparing the trust as well as probating the estate. Good estate planners no longer use testamentary trusts. If one is recommended to you, be sure you ask why a revocable living trust is not being prepared instead. If your lawyer can't explain the costs and benefits of wills and trusts, then you have the wrong lawyer.

CHAPTER TWO

You Must Have a Trust If . . .

Having a trust is advantageous for most people, and if they don't have one, the worst that can happen is that their estate gets probated, which takes a lot of time and costs the family a lot of money. A shame, but not the end of the world. However, for a lot of folks, a trust is an absolute necessity to protect their family's financial future. If any of the following applies to you, a trust is critical, and anyone who says you do not need one in any of these situations is flat-out wrong.

MINORS

If you do not have a trust and die while your children are still young, the inheritance will be given to them in a lump sum when they reach the "age of majority"—age eighteen in most states. In the meantime, the money is held in a court-supervised conservatorship account under the control of the minor's guardian or conservator. There are three things wrong with this.

First, in my experience turning over a lump sum of cash to an eighteen-year-old is a bad idea. I have seen it happen, and time and again, the money is wasted. In fact, leaving a large amount of money to an eighteen-year-old is actually a disincentive to getting an education. The child has never had any significant amount of money before, does not know how to manage it, and might think that going to college is not necessary with "all that money" in the bank. Unfortunately, the money soon disappears through bad management, poor decisions, and excessive spending on himself and his friends. I have seen a number of eighteen-year-olds inherit money that they no longer have at age nineteen or twenty. Then, when they do want to go to school, there is no way to pay for it.

The second problem is the court-supervised conservatorship. It sounds like a good idea to have a judge oversee the child's money, but in fact this can be a very complex and time-consuming process for the guardian who is acting as conservator of the money. Virtually every decision made by the conservator has to be approved by the judge. The money has to be put into restricted accounts over which the conservator has little investment control. In most jurisdictions, the conservator must prepare an annual accounting of income and expenses, prepare a written annual report, and appear in front of the judge for the judge's approval. Every year, and usually with a lawyer. True, we need oversight in some cases to be sure the conservator will not steal the money, but I find that the conservator is typically a grandparent, aunt, or uncle who would not steal from the child in a million years.

The third problem is that the guardian of the child is most often also the conservator of the money. Again, this seems logical, but often divorced parents tell me they want to be sure the other parent, the ex-spouse, does not end up in control of the child's money for one reason or another—usually because they do not trust the ex to use the money for the best interests of the child.

With a trust, you can set up rules as to when and how much money is given to a child and who will be in charge of that money.

Typical plans might include some of the following sorts of provisions:

1. All of the child's inheritance would be held in a trust fund under the control of a trustee chosen by the parent until the child reaches a certain age (for example, twenty-five). Until then, the trustee has the authority and the decision-making discretion to pay for such things as college tuition, books, transportation, medical expenses, or whatever the trustee believes to be a reasonable expense. The child does not decide what to spend the money on. The child can make requests, but the final decisions as to the appropriateness of the requests are those of the trustee.
2. Similar plans would give the child one-third the balance of the trust fund money at age twenty-five, one-third at age thirty, and one-third at age thirty-five—or a similar pattern. There may be authority to make additional distributions to the trust beneficiary if the trustee believes these are appropriate.
3. Some parents put conditions on the distribution of money, such as requiring drug screening of the beneficiaries before they are eligible for a payout. Other conditions can be put in the trust and do not have to be approved by anyone. Some I have seen (but do not necessarily agree with) set up requirements such as attending a particular college, staying a member of a particular church, maintaining a certain grade point average, acting as a missionary for a certain period of time, getting married by a certain age, and even not getting married before a certain age. There are so many more, limited only by a person's imagination.

The point is that a trust is flexible and can be set up with whatever rules and regulations you want. There are no guidelines so long as the terms are legal. And the money is yours to leave in whatever fashion you choose, regardless of what anyone else thinks. It's your stuff, not theirs.

DISABLED BENEFICIARIES

As we know, there are millions of disabled people. Disabilities may exist from birth or may be inflicted later on as a result of accident or illness. The mental or physical problems of an heir may require that someone else take care of the special needs of the person so that assets are used in the heir's best interests. The disabled person may be perfectly capable of making financial decisions, but leaving that right to them may mean they are disqualified from certain governmental benefits to which they would otherwise be entitled.

Physical or mental disabilities create two needs for a trust. First, the disabled may not have the mental or physical capacity to handle the ongoing management of their money. Bills need to be paid, money invested, taxes prepared. They may be subject to coercion or undue influence by those who would take the money they rely on, or they may just make bad money-management decisions. Having their inheritance left to them in trust, under the control of an independent trustee, solves this problem.

Second, leaving money to a disabled beneficiary is often like leaving them nothing at all. The reason is that many disabled people rely on state or federal benefit programs for their medical care. Medical care is, of course, very expensive, and most of us would go broke fast having to pay for it without insurance. Nursing-home care, for example, can cost in excess of $100,000 per year. A day in the hospital may cost thousands. Certain drugs are unaffordable without help.

Programs like Medicaid are what we call "need based." This means that the person needing help must qualify based on his or her income and assets. This varies by state because even though Medicaid is a federal program, each state administers the payout based on its own eligibility rules. Online you can find Medicaid eligibility for your state. One site is *http://www.medicaidoffice.net/medicaid-eligibility*. So if you leave money to a person who is receiving Medicaid, he may no longer qualify because of the amount of inherited money and must spend down the inheritance to the threshold level by paying for his own medical care. Then, when the money is gone, he has to go through the sometimes lengthy process of reapplying for the medical benefits.

I am not making a judgment of right or wrong here, but I can tell you that most people would prefer to leave money to their disabled beneficiaries in such as way as to not disqualify them from aid programs and still let them benefit from the inherited assets. A properly arranged "special needs" provision in your trust can do just that. This provision allows the money to be used for things that benefit them during their lifetime and then have the remainder go to some other beneficiary after death. The special-needs provisions have to be carefully written, since the wrong wording can completely throw out the intent of the provisions and make the inheritance subject to spend-down. Also, the beneficiary cannot be his or her own trustee.

SPENDTHRIFTS

We all know people who just cannot hold onto money. If they have it, they spend it. If they can borrow it, they will spend it. Their credit cards are maxed out. They may have declared bankruptcy, had repossessions, or even been sued for nonpayment of bills. These people are spendthrifts and will spend their inheritance very quickly if it is not protected for them. There are several ways to handle this, and a trust is ideal for managing their money. A trust can structure their inheritance in the following (and many other) ways:

1. **Allowance.** Leave them a share of the trust assets but have it given to them in a certain amount per month

so they do not get a lump sum to waste. Another provision could say where the remainder of the trust funds will go if they die before it is all given to them. A variation on this is to pay out only the interest on the trust funds, with the principal going to someone else—perhaps the grandchildren—at the death of the beneficiary.

2. **Set number of years.** A common method is to have an inheritance paid out in annual installments over five, ten, fifteen, or twenty years. The rationale here is that if the beneficiary makes a mistake with one installment, he will have time to think about it before the next installment comes along. It also solves the problem of someone entering a bad marriage or investing in a failing business and losing the inherited money along the way.
3. **Retirement accounts.** I see clients who have adult children who are not necessarily bad with money but have low-paying jobs with no retirement plans, have no savings, and therefore have no money for the future. The parents can set up a plan that pays out a percentage at their death with the balance held in trust and invested for them until the beneficiary reaches retirement age—say, sixty-five or sixty-six. Alternatively, if they should become permanently disabled, the trust could be paid out as an annuity for life.

There are many other variations on distributions to spendthrifts that basically manage money for someone who cannot effectively manage it for herself. If you can put together a plan, your attorney can put it in the right legal language.

Similar considerations and plans need to be made for heirs who have substance abuse problems or who are incarcerated. Some states now will go after the assets of an inmate to pay for care.

GAY COUPLES/UNMARRIED COUPLES

An unmarried couple, whether gay or not, needs the protection only a trust can offer. Unmarried couples do not have the legal rights afforded to those who are married in most states. Here's an example: Allen came to see me after his partner William died. They had been together for eighteen years. William had three adult children who seemed to get along with Allen—in fact, they exchanged presents for birthdays and Christmas. Now that William was dead, the relationship had changed and the children were no longer so fond of Allen. It seems the house they lived in was originally William's. They had both paid their share of the mortgage and shared all the other expenses of the house, but Allen's name had never been put on the title. Now that William was gone, the kids wanted the house. Neither Allen nor William had made out a will or a trust. Allen had no legal rights to live in his own home any longer. This meant that the kids could (and did) rightfully and legally evict Allen. I have also seen the same thing happen several times in heterosexual relationships. While mom or dad is alive, everything is fine, but once death removes them, the family relationship quickly turns into a matter of money. The moral is to get some written protection for your partner in your trust documents.

With a trust, you can provide your partner with the right to live in the house for his or her lifetime—what we call a life estate or life lease. At your partner's death, the kids can sell the house. Or you can provide that the partner has a right to live there for a set period of time, such as one or two years. Often there is a requirement that the bills have to be paid, such as mortgage, taxes, insurance, and maintenance, in order to have the right to stay in the house. Sometimes provisions are put in that would not allow the surviving partner to rent the house or share it with others. The choice of restrictions and requirements is yours.

Other issues arise such as determining ownership of furniture and other personal property items, and provisions for these should be specifically set out in the trust language. Either partner could make a list of individual items to be given immediately at death to particular people, with the rest of the household goods and furniture going to the survivor. One of the purposes and goals of a well-written trust is to avoid problems for surviving partners and beneficiaries. We do this by having an answer to the "what if" questions and making the trust provisions totally unambiguous.

BLENDED FAMILIES

In the typical family unit today, one or both partners may have been previously married and they may both have children from those prior marriages. Estate planning is an absolute must in these situations. Otherwise, everything may end up in the hands of the children of the spouse who lives the longest when that may not have been the intent of the couple.

The first consideration is to be sure your current spouse is protected by the trust provisions. Often, the marital home was owned before the marriage by one spouse or the other. It is not unusual to find the new spouse's name was never put on the title to the property—a big problem, since the new spouse may have to probate the house in order to continue to live in it and may even find that the stepchildren own all or part of it. Having the house in the name of the marital trust assures that the surviving spouse will be able to continue to live in the house without interference from the family.

The second factor is survival. Without a trust or will, the assets will, in most cases, belong to the surviving spouse. At her death, those assets would by law go to her children. So without a trust, it could become a gamble—a matter of who lives the longest—to determine whose children get the joint assets.

A trust can contain very flexible provisions to meet your intentions. For example:

1. At the death of one spouse, an immediate distribution of certain assets or money is made to that person's chil-

dren, with the rest staying in trust for the benefit of the survivor.

2. At the death of one spouse, the income from the marital trust assets could be paid out to the survivor as they are earned, with the remainder at death paid out to all the children of both spouses.
3. The trust could become unchangeable at the death of one spouse to insure that the children of the first spouse to die are not disinherited by the survivor. This means, in effect, that the trust becomes irrevocable at the first death.
4. Most commonly the surviving spouse gets the use and ownership of all the trust assets but cannot change the trust to effectively disinherit the children of the first spouse to die.

Any rules that you think are fair and both agree on can be put into the trust rules and regulations. The above are just a few examples. The point is that if you do not decide now, then state law will decide for you—and you may not like what the law would do. Keep in mind that if you and your spouse have a premarital agreement, the terms of that agreement may have to be modified to fit the above examples.

SEPARATED COUPLES OR SEPARATE TRUSTS

Sometimes both spouses don't agree on what would go into a joint trust and want separate plans funded with their own separate assets. Especially if a couple is separated, each would want to be certain that the trust is not going to be invaded after the death of the first by the survivor. In most states, if both parties agree, the trust assets in separate trusts are not reachable by the survivor except as specifically spelled out in the trust documents. The trust becomes in effect a postnuptial agreement.

With a will, a surviving spouse has rights over and above what the will of the deceased partner set out. In Michigan, for example, there are rights of election, homestead allowances, and exempt property rights—all of which allow a surviving spouse to "break" the will. So, in effect, you cannot disinherit a spouse with a will. You may write a will that says your spouse is supposed to get a certain amount, but the spouse has the right, through probate court, to take what the state would give instead of what the will provides.

A trust does not have that problem in many states, particularly if both spouses agree in writing to abide by the trust terms. This can be done by including the right language in the trust and then having the trust signed by both parties. Beware, however, of one partner fraudulently misrepresenting the nature and extent of his assets to get the other to agree. A court may then set aside the agreement.

In Michigan and some other states, at least under current law, a surviving spouse cannot elect against a trust and is stuck with whatever he or she is given under the terms of the trust. There are no other options. A trust is a much safer way of assuring that your instructions will be followed.

LARGE ESTATES

Trusts can eliminate or dramatically reduce estate and inheritance taxes. You might think you do not need to worry about estate tax since the threshold at the time of this writing is $5.45 million, but keep in mind that the IRS considers all assets taxable. So life insurance, retirement plans, and real estate, as well as traditional investments, are considered taxable. I have seen young parents with very little in the way of liquid assets who have multimillion-dollar life insurance policies (which are taxable for estate tax purposes at their deaths) and who ended up paying a huge estate tax bill that could have been avoided with a trust.

This is important because it is a big tax. The tax rate is effectively forty percent of everything over the threshold (though the rate is also subject to legislative change). So a $6 million estate could have a tax bill of $220,000.

A typical marital trust can have provisions that double the estate tax exemption amount, effectively preserving two exemptions. Under the current rules, a joint trust (or reciprocal trusts) would be nontaxable up to $10.9 million. This is a very inexpensive way of saving potentially huge amounts of tax, without complicating things while you are alive. Some estate planning attorneys are unaware of the type of joint trust that can preserve two estate tax exemptions. Warning: if you have just over $5.45 million and your attorney pushes the complex two-trust plan while being unable to explain why the joint trust with tax exemption doubling alternatives is unavailable to you, perhaps you are speaking to the wrong attorney.

Also keep in mind that this is not a tax advice book. Taxes are complex and often change. State laws may allow taxation of your estate even though there is no federal tax, so get good advice.

Large estates can also achieve significant estate and income tax savings using the more sophisticated types of trusts, such as charitable remainder trusts, as well as family limited partnerships, limited liability companies, and other complex estate planning techniques. Consult an estate planning expert to develop a plan for you.

Remember that Congress changes the tax laws frequently, so you should keep track of the exemption amount as it may be significantly different from what it was when this book went to press. (There is a good chance that the federal estate tax will be eliminated entirely, which would be a big loss of business for tax planning attorneys—stay tuned.) Having the joint trust with the tax provisions would, however, give you twice the then-current exemption amount, so it is the safest way to go, even if you think you are likely to fall under the single exemption amount.

SMALL ESTATES

Even some very small estates benefit from having a trust. You should refer to chapter 9, where I discuss small estates, but in some cases a trust is called for even if non-trust alternatives are available. For example, you may have only your house, a small savings account, and a life insurance policy to leave your children at your death. These could be handled without a trust and without probate by devices such as joint ownership and beneficiary designations.

But suppose you have one of the categories of concerns I covered earlier, such as a disabled child, an unmarried partner, an unequal distribution plan among children, or spendthrift heirs? You can, by using a trust, see that the money available is used for specific purposes, like paying off a child's education loans or tuition or holding it for them until they meet certain conditions you set up. And remember the problem with a person receiving assets that may disqualify him or her from receiving Medicaid or other need-based benefits. I have had a number of clients who were estranged from their children and even some who have children in prison. They may not want these children to share in the estate, and a trust can easily accomplish this intent. Trusts can be a way of making maximum use of a limited amount of money.

I have had people tell me that they are concerned about the cost of probate in their small estate because of the amount of cost relative to the size of the estate. Paying three or four thousand dollars for probate may be affordable for a $500,000 estate but may seem like a large share of a $100,000 one—especially if there are a lot of heirs. I have seen cases where the attorney got a bigger share of the estate than did the individual beneficiaries after all the probate costs were figured. This should not happen with a trust.

DISABILITY

A trust and its related documents avoid the need for court-ordered adult guardianship and conservatorship. A legal guardian is the person who is in charge of caring for a disabled adult, whether due to mental or physical disability, to the point that the person cannot take care of himself. This is done under the authority of the probate or family court and requires a fairly complex legal process. A petition is filed either by a social agency or family member stating the need for the guardianship. The court appoints an independent lawyer, a "guardian ad litem" (GAL) for the allegedly incapacitated individual—the ward. This procedure and the terminology will vary state by state, but the process is similar.

The GAL interviews the ward and others who have knowledge about the ward, reports back to the court in writing, and usually appears in person at a court hearing. All relatives are notified and can attend the hearing or bring their own attorneys. The judge then decides whether the guardianship is needed and, if so, appoints a guardian who from then on has to report to the court in writing and in person on how the ward is doing. The estate of the ward has to pay the guardianship fees.

A conservator—a person appointed by a court to manage the money of another person—is usually appointed at the same time. Minor children may have conservators. Disabled adults may also have conservators. The purpose of the conservatorship is to be sure that the ward's (the person who is in need of the conservatorship) money is being honestly and effectively managed. This is a valuable service for the ward, but it comes at a high cost to the family. Often the guardian and the conservator are different people, not family members, and both are paid from the assets of the ward.

In order to establish a conservatorship for an adult, an interested party petitions the court. This may be a family member, a state agency such as Adult Protective Services, or even a concerned nonfamily member. This person or agency states in writing why he or she believes the ward needs a conservator. The court then appoints a GAL, typically an attorney or county agency, who visits the ward, investigates the situation, then reports back to the court with a recommendation on whether a conservatorship is needed. Then there is usually a court hearing.

Family members and others can testify under oath as to the facts they know relating to the mental state of the ward, giving examples of what the ward may be doing to cause the need for someone else to take over.

This is often a humiliating experience for the ward and embarrassing to the family. The expense is high because the ward has to pay the GAL even if the conservatorship is found to be unnecessary, and the family may have to hire one or more other attorneys to promote their view of the conservatorship.

It doesn't stop there. If the conservatorship is granted, the conservator charges additional annual fees for acting as conservator. Further, the assets of the ward may have to be placed in restricted accounts with little opportunity for the best investment management. The conservator has to account to the court annually for everything financial that is done and may even need individual permission for extraordinary expenses of the ward.

All this is avoided with a trust. The trust has language that defines when a person is to be considered incapacitated, and when that occurs, the alternate or successor trustee immediately steps in and begins managing the assets of the trust owner. When combined with the medical directives and power of attorney that are part of the trust-based estate plan (see chapter 12), there is no need for a court-supervised guardianship and conservatorship. In fact, I have defeated petitions for guardianship in court merely by showing the judge that the proposed ward already had a durable power of attorney and medical power of attorney, as well as a revocable trust with a trustee in place managing the assets.

If you have any of the concerns outlined above, you absolutely must have a trust or the inherited assets are likely to be wasted or misused.

CHAPTER THREE

A Comparison: Trusts and Wills

Okay, so what is the truth? Is a will the best choice because it's cheaper? Is it cheaper?

At an estate planning seminar recently, I discussed trusts versus wills with another attorney. He was of the opinion that there was no cost-saving at all in having a trust instead of a will, even if probate was avoided. Therefore, his advice to all but the rich was to use a will. I was very interested in how he arrived at that conclusion.

His reasoning was as follows: He charged a lot of money for the will up-front (so he was not talking about a $250 simple will). His estate plan package using a will plus the durable power of attorney and medical directives was approaching $1,500. He then charged a lot for probate (with his fees at $300 per hour over a year or two of probate for a modest estate, the total would easily cost $5,000 to $10,000).

So does that support my argument for avoiding probate and using a trust? Well, no. He also charged a lot for a trust—typically $2,500 to $3,500. Then he charged a lot for what he called "trust settlement"—again at $300 per hour—and it took a long time to complete the process since his office did virtually everything to carry out the trust terms, many of which were not legal services. So using this lawyer saved no money or time at all. He was creating a huge fee no matter how the estate was handled. In his case, he was right: there was no advantage to the trust.

More on avoiding this kind of lawyer in chapter 5.

A very nice trust that will meet nearly everyone's needs can be had for a very reasonable price—much less than Mr. Lawyer was charging in the previous paragraph. You have to do your homework, interview lawyers, get referrals, go to seminars—all the techniques for finding the right lawyer I outline in chapter 5. If you do that, you will find that the initial cost of setting up the trust is practically the only legal fee you will ever pay for your estate plan. The reason is that trust settlement is not legal work. It is mostly clerical work. You do not need to pay $300 an hour to a lawyer to settle a trust if you know what to do.

Trust settlement is the process of carrying out the instructions in the trust as to who gets what and when. The typical chores must be done of identifying what debts have to be paid, publishing notice in the newspaper, getting an IRS number to open a bank account, selling assets, filing claims for life insurance, and so forth, but these are not legal work and do not require a lawyer.

What you need are instructions to the trustee upon death of the trust owner. Most lawyers are not going to give these instructions to you. They keep this process a secret. But I am going to tell you how to do it step by step in this book's final chapter. In fact, in every trust-based estate plan I have done, there is a section on trustee instructions, which, if followed, allow a quick and easy settlement of the trust with no legal costs at all. Am I shooting myself in the foot? True, I don't charge for trust settlement very often, but I have plenty to do creating trusts by referral from satisfied clients.

Using a will and probating it, however, is definitely legal work; plus, it is time consuming and therefore expensive. Most people cannot do their own probate. True, much of it is computerized, using software packages and fill-in-the-blank forms, but only lawyers have these or know how to use them. The probate system and probate laws are also geared toward making it take a long time. Completing a standard probate case in less than six months is nearly impossible because of the way the system is set up with its waiting periods, notice and publication requirements, and oftentimes court hearings that may be required.

Probate is an attorney's bread and butter—kind of like the slot machines that pay the rent in Vegas.

In fact, if you live in a state like California or Florida, the laws do not even allow you to do probate without a lawyer. They say that every personal representative (think executor) must be represented by a lawyer. So you couldn't do it yourself, even if you wanted to. Most everybody subject to probate in those states should have a trust.

It used to be, and still is in some states, true that probate had one advantage that trusts did not: a short statute of limitations. This means that by publishing a notice in the local newspaper to potential creditors of the deceased, you can limit how long any creditor has to present a claim against the probate estate to four, six, or nine months, depending on state law.

Years ago, other attorneys and I would intentionally put parts of certain estates through probate just to get this short statute of limitations. For example, say I represented the estate of a deceased surgeon. We would not want the estate held open and subject to possible lawsuits for malpractice until the normal negligence statute of limitations expired in maybe a year or two. By having part of his estate probated, we could shut the door on any possible claims that might be out there and get the estate finalized. The rest of the estate would be handled by the trust.

I don't worry about that anymore. In 2010, Michigan joined many other states in adopting a form of the Uniform Trust Act, which gives trusts the same sort of protection wills have always enjoyed. So now we never probate estates for statute of limitation reasons. Included in my set of instructions to the trustee in the last chapter is a fill-in-the-blank publication notice that the trustee runs one time in the newspaper to get the four-month statute of limitations for the trust, thereby canceling the only advantage of probate over trusts. You might want to use this even if your state does not officially recognize the validity of the trust notice publication as a way of identifying unknown creditors.

The availability of publication to shorten the statute of limitations may not exist in your state. If you are like most people, the danger of having a claim presented after the trust is settled is slim to none. Most of us know what the debts are. However, if you are in a high-risk occupation or have been involved in numerous business dealings that might or could lead to litigation, and you are in a state where the trust notice doesn't have a statute of limitations protection, having one small part of your estate probated will give you that protection. The rest of your assets can pass through the trust.

Sometimes there are problems in trusts that require a judge to sort them out, but not often. It is very rare for a trust to end up in court; however, if a trustee needs the assistance of the court for some reason, the probate court has the authority to administer and oversee trusts on request of an interested party.

REAL ESTATE IN MORE THAN ONE STATE

It is not unusual to see people who own real estate in multiple states, such as a winter home in Florida and a summer home in the north. With a will, probate would be necessary in both states. No state has the authority to probate real estate located in another state. Without a trust, probate would have to be done in each state where real estate was located. So we have for a New York resident what is called "ancillary probate" in Florida, which is basically a companion probate. It then effectively doubles the cost of probate. I had a client with real estate in five different states—big trouble without a trust. And ancillary probate can be expensive. The attorney handling it had no relationship with the family, was not likely to see any of their business again, and therefore charged the maximum going rate for the probate.

With a trust, all the real estate from every state can be put into one trust ownership using a quitclaim deed and there is no probate in any state. The trustee merely hires an attorney in the companion state to do a deed from the trust to the beneficiaries, or the trustee sells the property in the other state through the trust. No probate and no expenses other than realtor and closing fees.

Huge savings in time, trouble, and money. Those of you with real estate in more than one state need a trust.

FAMILY HARMONY

Wills can cause family trouble. There are two reasons for this. First, probate takes a long time to complete, from several months to several years depending upon what problems arise. Because of this time delay, heirs become suspicious of the executor and the attorney for the estate. I have heirs come to see me who think they should have their own lawyer in the probate just to protect their interests. They ask me, "How do I know for sure that the executor is doing the right things without somebody on my side?"

When you get two or more lawyers involved, the costs begin to go up. You are paying a lawyer for results. They want to appear to be doing something for you, so they bill hours, write letters, do research, and make telephone calls. Law is a game of adversaries with each lawyer fighting for his or her client. It causes trouble, expense, and hard feelings. Your lawyer is not doing his job unless he can point to something he accomplished. It may be that all he has to do is monitor the proceedings, but that is not the way it usually works out.

Second, wills are fairly easy to contest. When a probate case is opened, a court file number is given to it, a judge is assigned to the case, and easy-to-use court forms are made available for filing motions and setting up hearings. Attorney fees are what the court calls priority claims. In other words, the lawyers get paid first, so there is a pot of money out of which attorneys can collect their fees. Attorneys do not expect a big up-front retainer in a will contest.

Contesting a trust is a different matter, however. Attorneys will expect a retainer fee and bill against that at their normal hourly rates, win or lose. Having to come up with a lot of cash is a disincentive to contesting a trust.

This ease of contesting a will leads to will contest extortion. Executors often settle a specious claim against a will just because it is often cheaper and quicker than trying to fight over it. There are some—not many, but some—lawyers who engage in this blackmail game and are rarely called on it. There are court rules that are supposed to prevent this from happening, but they are not often enforced.

Remember that the cost of probate is not what lawyers would lead you to believe. It is not the state, the court system, taxes, or "court costs" that run up the cost of probate. It is almost entirely attorney fees.

On the other hand, trust settlement without an attorney can be done quickly and with no legal costs. Because everything is wrapped up so fast, there is not much time for heirs to worry about the process. You basically gather together the assets, pay the bills, publish notice, file the last year's income tax return, and distribute the assets to the heirs—that's it. No papers to file with a court or the state, and no fees to pay.

No-contest clauses and arbitration clauses also limit challenges to trusts. A no-contest clause is a paragraph or two that says that anyone who challenges the trust, even if they are successful, would get only one dollar as their inheritance. While this clause is not a bar to challenging a trust on the basis that the maker of the trust was senile or otherwise incompetent when they made the trust, the fact that the provision is there stops a lot of trust contests. It's kind of like the sign in the parking garage that says they are not responsible for loss or damage to your car. The sign itself discourages people from suing even if the garage might actually be legally responsible.

Similarly, an arbitration provision can slow down contests. This provision says that if someone wants to challenge the trust or any part of it, they must first submit to arbitration to settle their claim and if unsuccessful must pay for the arbitration fees of both sides. That one is a real stopper. Arbitration is like a mini-trial of all the issues. It can cost a lot, it can take a lot of time, and the outcome is uncertain. Plus there is the no-contest provision that may be enforceable, so even if the other side wins, they may get nothing. Personally, I like this arbitration provision.

To contest a trust, the one contesting must hire and pay for a lawyer out of her own pocket. There is no probate court priority for attorney fees, and it can be difficult to find a lawyer willing to take on a trust contest on a contingency fee basis (getting their attorney fees out of the winnings). Trusts are a more certain way of seeing that your intentions and instructions are carried out at death and are not thwarted by litigation.

PRIVACY

Probate files are public record. Many people are not aware of this, but anyone can go to the courthouse, look at any court file, and find out who inherited what and how much they got. I heard of a car dealer years ago who gleaned the names of heirs from probate files so he could try to sell them cars. "I hear you came into some money. I have a heck of a deal on a new Cadillac for you." Seems sleazy, but it is perfectly legal.

A trust is private. No one other than the heirs knows what anyone inherited, what restrictions there might be, or even the size of the estate. Most of us want this information private, and a trust keeps it that way. (Although if, in that one-in-a-hundred case, the trust gets filed with the court, then it can be made public record too.)

The privacy aspect also makes it harder to contest because only the named heirs involved can get a look at the paperwork.

CHAPTER FOUR

Trust Seminars: A Free Dinner, But at What Cost?

Because of my age, I think, at least every other week I receive an invitation by mail or telephone to attend a free dinner at a local hotel or restaurant. These folks seem to have the AARP mailing list. The invitation is typically from a stockbroker, financial planner, attorney, or estate planner. The point of the dinner is ostensibly to give me information important to me on estate taxes, guardianships, how to avoid probate, taking care of my IRAs, and so on.

I actually go to some of these dinner seminars just to see what people are being told and what they are being sold. Most of them are in the same vein—a Power Point presentation narrated by up to three speakers for the purpose of convincing the audience that they need to get their financial affairs and estate planning in order—or else! Some of them have exaggerated claims of the time and expense of probate to scare people into signing up with them. Some have information that is downright incorrect. I attended one seminar run by an attorney who was so far off base in his advice that I was tempted to stand up in the back of the room and tell the audience not to listen to this guy because he did not know what he was talking about.

Everyone at the seminars eventually figures out that the agenda of the presenters is to sell something. Whether it is long-term care insurance, brokerage services, legal documents, or annuities, they are not feeding you for nothing. They want your money.

I am reminded of my mother, who has a closet full of umbrellas and tries to give me one every time I visit.

"Where did you get all these umbrellas?" I asked the first time.

She replied, "The Buick dealer down the street gives me an umbrella and a hot dog every Sunday if I take a test drive."

Mom was never going to buy a Buick and I think the dealer knew that, but sales is a numbers game—get in front of enough people and some will buy. It's the same thing with these seminars. Some people go to all the ones they are invited to just to get the free meal. But some of the guests are new and some of them eventually get convinced.

I have been approached by a number of companies over the years that put on these seminars. They ask me if they can refer their customers to me to prepare a trust-based estate plan for them. I have to very carefully investigate companies making such requests. Some are good, and some are downright crooked. As a consumer, you have to be cautious with whom you deal in financial and legal matters, particularly when you are revealing your personal financial and family information to them.

So here is the criterion you should look at in deciding whether to attend a trust seminar:

Who is putting on the seminar? Attorneys may hold workshops or seminars as a way of attracting new clients. The information is usually good, and it is the attorneys' services for preparing a trust, powers of attorney, and funding services that are being sold. The attorney cannot sell annuities or insurance, so you are not going to be pressured on those fronts. He may try to get you to sign up for an office conference or may even visit you in your home to wrap up the details.

What to watch out for: just because they are putting on a seminar does not mean they know what they are doing or are charging you a fair price. See the next chapter on attorneys for more about that. Check out the attorney: How long has he been in practice? How many trusts does he do every year? How long will it take to get the trust done? Be sure you have a written fee agreement and that you know in advance what the total costs will be. Do not agree to an hourly rate. An agreed-upon flat rate for the entire service should be in writing.

Are you a member of a prepaid legal services plan? Some attorneys participate in these plans and can do all of your estate planning at no cost to you. In my office, for example, you get exactly the same documents and services if you have legal insurance as you would if you were paying cash. I have seen some attorneys, though, that give their clients the stripped-down version if it's through a legal plan.

Brokers, financial planners, and insurance agents will discuss living trusts, guardianships, and so forth—and may even have an attorney to whom they refer you—but their primary goal is to sell you annuities, long-term care insurance, or other investments. They may want to sign you up as a client and charge a fee for financial planning advice. Often they want to rework your IRA. Remember that they make a commission on anything they do, and be sure that you are getting advice based on your best interest rather than the agent's. Be certain that any change they make in your investments, including your IRAs and retirement accounts, is not going to reduce the value of that account or put unacceptable restrictions on your access to your own funds. A good way of protecting yourself is to listen to what they have to say and then run their recommendations past another person in the same business. The money you have now is not easily replaced if lost in a bad investment, especially when you are retired.

Trust sales companies are a mixed bag. Seminars are being run throughout the country by big organizations to sell you on a living trust and all the related documents. The presentations are slick and the sales techniques are high pressure. There are sometimes no local attorneys involved in the preparation of the legal documents at all—often the legal work is done in another state by the company employees and then shipped back to the salesman for delivery to you. The trusts are generic, not necessarily appropriate for you, hard to understand, and overpriced. I know all this because I have seen dozens of these trusts brought to me for a review of validity.

Beware of any company that claims it is selling you legal documents if the people are not themselves attorneys. It is illegal in most states for a nonattorney to give legal advice, to prepare an estate plan for you, or to sell legal documents specifically designed for you. They may say attorneys are preparing the documents, but if the attorney fees are included in what you pay them, this is illegal, unethical, and may involve no attorney at all.

Illegally selling you legal documents at an inflated price is not the end of it. They use the trust as a way of getting you to reveal all your personal financial information and then try to sell you investments on which they receive big commissions. Some of these companies have been prosecuted for tactics like these, but they often just open up under another name and keep going. The free dinner is not worth the risk of being talked into a bad deal. These salespeople are very convincing.

Trust service companies are different from the trust sales companies and are up-front and completely reputable. A trust service company is not selling you a trust. It may offer you a list of local attorneys from which you can choose to discuss preparing a trust for you, but it does not prepare any legal documents itself or give legal advice. You can use your existing trust with them or even use your own attorney.

What you buy from these companies is typically a service package wherein they agree to help you "fund" your trust (see chapter 8), meet with you annually to be sure your trust is still properly funded, help you fill out a request to amend your trust (which you can send to your attorney to make changes you may want), and even assist the family after your death in submitting claims for life insurance and rolling over retirement plans.

Is their service worth what they charge? It depends, of course, on how good you are at keeping track of your assets yourself. In my experience, as I discuss later, trusts are less likely to be fully funded the older they are, so part of the estate sometimes ends up being probated even when there is a trust. However, with the trust service companies, which provide an annual review, it is rare to have any assets left out at death that need to be probated.

Keep in mind that you are not buying legal documents from a trust service company. They are not lawyers and cannot give legal advice, act as agents for a lawyer, or sell you legal documents. You are buying their services. Also, they sell things such as long-term care insurance and annuities, but you are under no obligation to buy anything at all from them or to let them manage any of your investments or assets. Get a second opinion before you transfer your IRA or 401(k) or buy an annuity or investment from anyone, especially someone coming to your home. That is always your choice. Be careful of companies that lead you to believe the fees you are paying them are for a trust. The attorney is the only one who can do the trust and will charge you separately for those services.

Check out the company you are thinking of dealing with. Call the Better Business Bureau. Ask for references from other customers they may have serviced. Be sure that you have a signed contract specifying exactly what you are paying for and that you have the right to a "cooling off" period, during which you have the right to cancel while you think it over.

I recommend that you also involve your adult children, if any, in order that they can understand what you have done and what their role will be at your death. Have one or more of the children present when you go over your legal documents. A reputable company or attorney will not discourage the children's participation.

On seminars, my view has always been that I am looking for education and information. Whether I buy anything or make an appointment for more information is secondary and requires a lot of thought and investigation. The same should be true of hiring an attorney.

CHAPTER FIVE

Watch Out for Attorneys

I will make two points in this chapter: the role of attorneys in preparing your estate planning and their role in wrapping up your estate at your death. Both require careful consideration on your part to avoid complications, time delays, and excessive cost to you and your heirs.

Attorneys play a vital role in planning your estate, and it would be a mistake to try to avoid them. True, you may be able to put together a trust from something you download off the Internet or from forms you buy at the office supply or book store, but you would have no assurance that what you have done is going to be legally sufficient and accomplish the goals you have in mind. In particular, the online forms may be specific to the state in which they are sold, and you have no idea who created them or if they will work for you. I am always amazed that people will risk everything they have acquired by putting it into a form from a book—without having expert legal advice—in order to save a bit of money. The old penny-wise-pound-foolish mistake.

The need for independent legal advice is why I have not included fill-in-the-blank forms in this book. There is no one trust that is right for everyone. We all have differing intentions, goals, finances, family relationships, and problems. In my office, I use computers of course but have developed about sixty separate trust formats for differing situations. Even so, I always have to adapt each one for each client's particular circumstance. I have included a comprehensive decision-making form in the appendix, which will be invaluable to your attorney because it customizes your decisions to your particular situation so that your documents fit you perfectly.

How to choose the attorney and what to watch out for are very important. I see too many people who do not ask questions, assuming that because the attorney has a law license she will not only know about trusts and estate planning but will treat them fairly. Sometimes true but not always. I see a lot of very poorly made trusts done by attorneys who I am sure the clients paid in good faith. I also see the same trust brought to me by different clients for review, so I know they are using a template. Sometimes the template trust is outdated and contains references to laws and legal situations that no longer exist. So be careful with whom you deal.

There are also advantages to having the guidance of an attorney through all phases of your lifelong estate planning and in assisting your family in wrapping up your estate. With regular contact, the attorney (if he is doing the right things for you) can be sure that your trust reflects your current wishes, takes care of you in case of disability, and provides for an orderly and efficient distribution of your assets at your death. These services come with a cost, but a good lawyer will make the investment worthwhile. Of course, you have to have a good lawyer to begin with and would be wise to know what to watch out for in hiring one, so here are my tips and warnings, gathered from having an inside view since 1975 of attorney practices.

WHAT ARE LEGAL SERVICES?

Lawyers charge a lot of money for what they do, but for the legal things that only a lawyer can do, these fees are not necessarily unreasonable. Only a licensed attorney can give specific legal advice, represent a person in court, or prepare legal documents. For these services, attorneys receive years of training and education, which justify the fees charged. They also assume responsibility for the rightness of their legal services and can be sued for attorney malpractice if they are wrong.

Nonattorneys cannot legally do any of those three things for other people. The problem in the estate planning area is that many of the services attorneys charge for are not legal services—they are clerical services. You pay for the attorney's time whether she is in court or just talking to you on the telephone, so your legal fees for the trust could be inflated because of these additional charges. For example, assistance in funding your trust is not all legal in nature. Changing the beneficiary on life insurance so that the trust is the beneficiary rather than a person can be done by anyone. Should you pay hundreds of dollars an hour to have an attorney request a beneficiary change form from the insurance company and fill it out for you? This is clerical work, not legal work. I suggest that when you interview your attorney, you ask to do some of the nonlegal work yourself if you want to save some money. Same with changing beneficiaries on retirement accounts and annuities—you can do this yourself with no legal assistance.

I know attorneys who will do all the trust funding for a client and charge the normal attorney fee rate for doing it. They have the client sign a power of attorney allowing them to access their financial affairs, then they contact the client's banks, credit unions, brokers, and insurance companies to see that all the assets get into the trust. This is a great service but not something you cannot do yourself with the right instructions. I provide my clients with trust-funding instructions so they can do the funding without paying me extra.

Trusts are so common nowadays that the financial institutions know what you need to do and will in most cases do the funding paperwork for you. Trust service companies can assist in the funding as can your financial planner or accountant. You do not have to pay the lawyer to do these things. If saving money on attorney fees is not important to you, then go ahead and let the lawyer do it—but know that you are paying attorney fee rates for clerical services.

WHEN YOUR WILL IS WORTHLESS

Clients often call the lawyer's office because they have been told that they should have a will. Everybody should have a will, people say, and if you do not have one, it is because you are procrastinating or are negligent or uncaring toward your family. That is the common feeling, but of course it is not necessarily true; in fact, few people actually need a will. Many need a trust, as we know from the information in this book, but wills are often superfluous if there is no trust.

The most common example I see is the situation where a lawyer prepares a will for a client, which is of no value at all. State laws have what they call laws of "intestacy." This means a set of laws that determine who inherits a person's property if he dies without a will or trust.

Typically, if a person dies leaving no spouse, his children share equally in whatever the deceased owned at death after all expenses are paid. If a will is made out saying that all the assets are to be divided equally among the children, then the will has accomplished nothing. Whether with a will or without, the estate would have to go through probate. Having a will does not make probate simpler, cheaper, or shorter. So in this case, the attorney who makes a will that mirrors the intestacy laws is charging the client for nothing. A married couple usually own everything jointly so that the surviving spouse automatically inherits everything without any court involvement, so there is nothing to probate at the death of one of them.

A trust can take care of every estate planning decision a person might want to make, whereas a will can be "broken." As we have already covered, a surviving spouse has a right to choose between what a will gives him and what state law would give if there was no will. So you can't disinherit your spouse in most states with a will, but you might be able to do so with a trust. The value of a will is that it gives directions as to the disposition of your estate that may be different than what the state law would do. *But* a trust is better because it does not have to be probated.

Some things may be put in the will that would not be covered by intestacy, which would make the will valuable, such as an unequal distribution among children or disinheriting a child. As explained earlier, a will can contain all the provisions to set up a testamentary trust. But wills have to be probated and trusts do not, so there is no advantage to the will.

I had a client come in asking for advice about her mother's trust. After that was finished, I asked her what plans she had made for her own estate. She said she was all set—she had a will. After I explained the difference between wills and trusts, she said she had originally asked the lawyer for a trust but he told her that all estates had to be probated, so a will was all she could get. I was astounded at the incorrect advice and prepared a trust for her. I suspect that the attorney knew nothing about trusts but did know about wills and probate and did not want to lose a client. I also think his advice constituted legal malpractice.

HOW MUCH SHOULD A TRUST COST?

Putting a suggested cost for a trust into this book would not be a good thing to do. The cost of legal services varies by where you live, what services are actually being provided, and the attorney who is doing the work. Any price I might put in this book will not necessarily be accurate either where you live or when you read this, though some other books on trusts do give estimates ranging around $3,500, which may be right for your area—but may also be higher or lower than the average where you live.

The important point is for you to know in advance what you are paying and what services are being performed for that price. You should be able to get a flat fee for a set amount of services. If you require more services than are agreed upon, expect to be charged more. If there are parts of the process you can do yourself, such as getting beneficiary change forms or doing other parts of the trust funding, then you should expect to save some money. And be sure all the other documents that go along with a trust are included. These include a pour-over will, durable powers of attorney, medical directives, living wills, do-not-resuscitate directives for those who want them, transfer deeds, trust certificates, and letters to the named successor trustees. I have always used a flat fee, which also included instruction to the successor trustees so they would know what to do on the death of the trust maker. Those instructions are included in the appendix.

It is unlikely that a lawyer will tell you over the telephone what he charges for a trust, since there are so many different things that may enter into a price determination. That being said, certain trust service companies and financial planners have informal agreements with attorneys to reduce prices for referred clients with the understanding that the financial planner will provide some of the nonlegal services such as information gathering, notarization of documents, and trust funding. It is worth looking into.

Also, watch out for a practice I've seen used once in a while: a fee based upon how much the lawyer saves you in estate taxes. There are attorneys who use the standard marital "A/B" trust, which automatically doubles the estate tax exemption at the death of one spouse. They then run a calculation showing the estate taxes that would occur without that kind of trust and then base their fee on a percentage of the savings.

Sort of sounds okay if you figure estate taxes would be $250,000 without the trust and nothing with the trust. So paying the lawyer $25,000 to save $250,000 is a good deal, right? Wrong. The A/B trust being used to get this saving is the same one used by most attorneys charging a flat rate of $2,500. There is no special expertise being offered by the lawyer working on a percentage, and in my view, the big fee is excessive and unethical. But it still happens and most clients are none the wiser.

SELECTING A LAWYER TO DO YOUR TRUST

A referral from a satisfied client or a trusted financial planner is the best way. If you do not have either of those, then you need to interview your attorney based on the following factors.

Find an expert. While legally any attorney can prepare your trust, very few have any expertise in this area. In some states, the Bar Association can certify attorneys as experts or specialists in certain areas. Other states, like Michigan, do not accredit specialties at all. Get a specialist if you can.

It is possible for a nonspecialist to create a good trust. It is also a gamble on your part. The lawyer who tries to handle everything, including divorces, bankruptcies, criminal cases, real estate, personal injury, and estate planning is not likely to be as familiar with trusts as is the attorney who only does trusts and probate. The specialist can determine what you need, give you the right advice, and prepare your documents faster and usually cheaper than can the nonspecialist, who may have to research unfamiliar (to her) areas of law for you. Do not pay for the lawyer's education; find someone who already knows what to do.

Part of my legal practice is reviewing trusts prepared by other attorneys and writing opinion letters based on the review. I tell the clients what is right and wrong with their trust and, if there are problems, what needs to be done to correct them. I have reviewed hundreds of trusts over the years drafted by other attorneys, and frankly I am appalled by the poor quality of legal work that goes on.

My experience is that many attorneys are using fill-in-the-blank trust programs that they receive from bank trust departments, buy from legal document companies, or are given to them at seminars they attend. These are computer programs where the attorney fills in the names of the client, their children, the trustees, and other things specific to the client and then prints it up. Sometimes the programmed trust chosen by the attorney is not at all appropriate for the client's needs.

I remember several years ago a client brought her trust into my office and dropped it on my desk with a loud thump. It was in a large three-ring binder, about 350 pages long, all boilerplate. When I looked at it, I pointed out to her that the only places in the whole document where her name or the names of her children and trustee appeared were on page 1 and page 350. The rest was basically just filler. She wanted a new one she could understand. The new trust I prepared for her was twenty-seven pages long, and she understood it.

Some of the trust formats I see again and again. A local bank used to hand out computer disks and manuals with the trust they wanted attorneys to use. A lot of attorneys took them and still use them today. Of course the document named the bank itself as a cotrustee, but it was possible to edit that out of the document. One of the priciest attorneys in town used this trust and charged what I consider outrageous attorney fees for something she did not even write.

I am not suggesting that trusts prepared in this way are never any good. They may work perfectly well, and in fact, some of them were developed by experts in the field who are sharing these with other attorneys in the hope of improving the quality of legal work out there. I am just letting you know that your trust was likely not written just for you, and you should keep that in mind when you write the check.

There is no specific format for a trust. I can write a perfectly legal trust on one page, though I do not do that for a number of reasons. Trusts do not have to be notarized or even witnessed in some states (though we usually do both of these), so trusts can be made overly simple or overly complicated. I like to make them complete enough to cover what is reasonably likely to happen but not so complex as to make them incomprehensible and unusable.

Ask outright how many trusts the attorney has done in the past and how many he typically creates in a month. Ask him how many wills he makes. The wills should be a small fraction of the trusts if you are talking to the right attorney.

ADVERTISING AND WEBSITES

A lawyer's advertisement is written by the lawyer or his staff. It is an advertisement, not an endorsement by anyone. The lawyer with the biggest ad is not necessarily your best choice. I was one of the first attorneys to advertise in the United States back in 1977. It made the newspapers, since lawyers were previously prohibited from advertising. I had two years' experience and did a little of everything. Business boomed. I did not profess to be an expert and instead just listed the kinds of cases I could do. Other lawyers were furious, saying I was demeaning the legal profession. Actually, I think they did not like to see the apple cart upset. That all changed. The lawyers that criticized me for advertising began advertising themselves and now have the big full-page color ads for their firms.

Thirty-five years later when I retired, I no longer advertised. I had one line with my name and telephone number in the telephone directory, and that was all. My print directory had about twenty pages of full-page ads for other lawyers and hundreds of smaller display ads. None of those were in any way an indication of the quality of the attorney running the ad. What you can learn from the ads, though, is information such as how long the lawyer has been in practice and whether she concentrates on just estate planning or tries to do everything. Armed with that information, you can then proceed to interview to decide if she is right for you—kind of like dating.

Websites are another form of advertising. The Internet is a dangerous place to get information. I recently ran across an attorney website filled with information on trusts. The attorney advised that trusts could not reduce taxes (wrong), that lawyers still had to be paid at death (wrong again), that many people were better off with a will due to statute-of-limitations issues (wrong in many states), and that probate still had to be done in many cases to cover personal property (wrong in most states).

For the most part, lawyers' websites are written by lawyers, and the information in them may be true in the particular jurisdiction where the lawyer is located but probably does not apply to everyone everywhere. The lawyer, in fact, may be wrong in her facts altogether. Nobody checks the accuracy of these sites.

Sometimes I think some of them are written to steer people away from trusts and toward wills and probate, where the real money is. But viewing biographical information about the lawyer herself can be helpful in making a choice.

The lesson for you is not to take what is listed on a website as necessarily accurate information, even if it is a lawyer website.

TRICKS

Well, maybe not tricks, but practices attorneys engage in that may not be in your best interests.

"My lawyer said I do not need a trust. A will is just fine for me."

I hear this fairly often from clients who have been referred to me by financial planners and others. There are two reasons, I think, why an attorney would tell a client they do not need a trust.

The first is ignorance. Many attorneys have had no training in trusts at all, as they most likely only took one course on trusts and estates while attending law school. Trusts are a small part of that, and the course may have focused primarily on the history of trusts and the tax reasons for having a trust. Thus, the attorney might truly and honestly believe that trusts are for wealthy people who need to minimize or avoid estate and inheritance tax. They have not read chapter 2 of this book and do not realize the importance of trusts for most people.

The second reason is related to the first in a sense. Attorneys know how to make wills and how to probate an estate. Most do not know about trusts and have never settled an estate using a trust or acted as a trustee—I actually prepare trusts for other attorneys who are not familiar with them, giving them the document based on information from their clients. I am sure they take my name off everything when they present the package to the client.

There may be an element of self-interest in trying to develop and maintain a probate practice with some attorneys. As I stated in my introduction, attorneys are taught to build their probate practice with a will file and will safe. It may be cynical to suggest that a lot of attorneys specifically steer people toward probate rather than trusts just for the money involved, but I can assure you that some do.

How do you keep clients and build up your probate practice (which is very lucrative)? One traditional method is to have a will safe (a locking file cabinet where clients' original wills are kept). After the will-signing ceremony, the lawyer gives the client a nice photocopy and holds the original for safekeeping. At the death of the client, the executor has to go back to the lawyer to get the will for probate and nine times out of ten will hire the lawyer to do the probate. Good business. Some attorneys even have themselves written into the will as attorneys for the estate or as executors. Why do you think the will envelope has the law firm name, address, and telephone number on it? So the family will know who to call to do the probate. Again, good business.

Those attorneys who want to specialize in estate planning are better served by developing trust expertise so that they do the best job for their clients who in turn should refer others to them. This is becoming much more common as continuing education programs for attorneys are now focusing on using trust-based estate plans in many states.

MY WILL DOES NOT HAVE TO GO THROUGH PROBATE

I hear this a lot, particularly from older clients (my age). For some reason, a lot of people believe that a will does not have to be probated. Well, in some cases that may be true—for example, if one spouse dies and the couple's property is all jointly owned, there may be nothing separately owned by the deceased to probate. But at the death of the survivor, probate would be absolutely necessary for all the assets left in the survivor's name.

I had a client point out to me the specific language in the will that clearly said it did not have to be probated. Here is the paragraph:

"It is my strongest intent that my estate not be subject to supervised probate court administration, and I therefore direct that such intent be followed as permitted by the Michigan Estates and Protected Individuals Code, or as may be available under current law."

Sounds like no probate. But that is not what it really says. It says that the client does not want "Supervised Probate Court Administration." In Michigan, there are two basic ways to probate an estate: an informal procedure and a formal procedure. Saying you do not want the supervised administration just means that you want the unsupervised form. It is still probate, it still takes a long time, and it still costs a lot of money. Unsupervised, though, is easier for the lawyer. I think clients interpret this paragraph to mean what it seems to say rather than what it really means.

THE ATTORNEY ANNUAL REVIEW

I said before in the trust services section that an annual review is a good idea to keep the trust funded and up to date with a client's wishes. That was said in the context of a service, which provided that review for your lifetime for a one-time flat fee.

Paying an attorney for an annual review is not always necessary. I know there are attorneys who act like dentists, setting annual appointments for all their clients to go over their estate planning. In most cases, nothing needs to be done. That will be $300—see you next year!

But keeping your documents up to date and in line with your current circumstances is very important. It just doesn't have to be done annually. You should contact your attorney in the following situations:

1. Someone involved in the trust has died or has become disabled and is receiving governmental benefits.
2. You have changed your mind about who will get what after you die.
3. You have changed your mind about who will be in charge of your trust at your death or upon your disability.
4. You have new real estate to transfer into your trust and need to have a deed prepared (see chapter 8 on funding the trust).
5. Your financial situation has dramatically changed or you are starting a new business.

Most of the time, this is not going to be an annual event. You may have several years go by during which you need no changes to your legal documents. The forced annual review is typically not needed. A good lawyer will let you know if there are changes in the law that necessitate a change in your documents and planning.

THE WILL AS A WAY TO FUND THE TRUST

One of the really reprehensible things I have seen done (this is my opinion, attorneys, so don't sue me) in trust practice by lawyers is using the pour-over will as a way to fund the trust with no attempt to fund it during the client's lifetime.

A "pour-over will" is a will that says if there are assets left in your name at your death that are not either in your trust or that pass to your trust under some sort of beneficiary or pay-on-death designation, you want those assets to be given to your trust after probate is complete—in other words, to "pour over" into your trust to be handled like any other trust asset. So it is meant as a backup document, just in case you forget to fund your trust with something. To repeat: if your trust is fully funded, the pour-over will is never used.

But some lawyers view the pour-over will as the funding mechanism for the trust. They put nothing at all into the trust during your lifetime. It is unfunded. Then, at your death, they probate the pour-over will and transfer the assets to the trust, before taking care of settling the trust.

This is a great deal for the lawyer. She can charge for creating the trust, creating the will, probating the estate, and settling the trust. There are a lot of attorney fees there—it's like getting paid twice for the same thing.

When properly done, you should have a completely funded trust with no assets in the name of the deceased at death, and therefore no probate should be necessary. With the instructions to the trustee I have included in the last chapter, your trustee should not need a lawyer at all at your death and should have no legal expenses beyond the creation of the original trust and any amendments that were made since that time.

CHAPTER SIX

Trustees

A trustee is someone you can trust—someone who will take charge of your trust documents after your death and carry out your wishes. This person (or people) is typically one or more of your adult heirs or members of your family.

What does a trustee typically do? The trustee takes care of not only the financial things such as gathering together investments, insurance death benefits, and selling real estate but also the more mundane things like cleaning out the garage and basement, making funeral arrangements, doing your final income tax returns, and paying any leftover bills. So while it does take some time, most of these duties do not require the services of a lawyer. Following the instructions in this book will make the job quite easy for most trustees.

How can you be sure your trustee can be trusted? There are ways to be more certain your trustee will do the job faithfully and honestly. One good way is to name two trustees as cotrustees to act together, especially if it is a blended family in which each parent has a separate set of children. Taking one child from each side of the family creates a situation where they watch each other and are more likely to do things properly.

In situations where there are no trustworthy people with whom you are comfortable, you can name a bank trust department or, as a last resort, have a provision put in your trust that the trust is to be registered with the probate court for supervision. (The name of the court handling probate cases is different in some states. It may also be called a circuit court, superior court, or district court, but it is the court that handles the estates of deceased people.) Or, even better, have a provision in your trust to have the court appoint a trustee while "acting in a ministerial capacity" rather than assuming full control and supervision of the trust. Trust supervision by the court is something akin to probate and is to be avoided if possible.

The law calls a trustee a "fiduciary" and, as such, imposes on the trustee certain legal obligations. A trustee is bound by the terms of the trust but also by the state law governing fiduciaries.

For example, there is in most states a set of laws commonly known as the "Prudent Investor Rules." These basically say that a trustee must be conservative and careful in managing the assets of the trust. The trustee must not put the trust assets in jeopardy by making risky investments. The trustee has statutory obligations to keep good accounting records and keep the trust beneficiaries informed as to what is happening with the trust. You need an organized trustee who keeps good records, so it is very important to choose the correct trustee.

Years ago, it was common to choose professional trustees—usually the trust department of a local bank. That still happens, but typically for larger trusts. The problem with professional trustees, in my experience, is that they are not too willing to exercise their discretionary power to make distributions to beneficiaries.

As an example, I was contacted by a twenty-one-year-old college student who was the beneficiary of the trust of her deceased grandfather. The bank was the trustee, and the trust said that the beneficiary was entitled to use the money for "educational purposes" and any other expense that the bank thought appropriate. There was about $1.5 million in the trust account.

The student had requested money to buy a used car because she wanted to live off-campus in an area with no bus service. The bank refused to give her anything for a car, saying that was an inappropriate and noneducational expense. Had her parents been the trustees instead of the bank, she probably would have gotten the money since it was not, in my view, unreasonable.

Most people choose family members as trustees to simplify things and keep the costs down.

YOU (AND/OR YOUR SPOUSE) AS TRUSTEE

The trustee is the one who is in charge of the trust. In most cases, the grantor (the maker and owner of the trust) is his own trustee during his lifetime. Couples usually have joint trusts or are cotrustees. If one of the couple dies, the survivor usually remains the sole trustee until death or disability. But not necessarily—it depends upon circumstances. Sometimes in situations where each spouse has his or her own trust, the directions are to name the survivor plus one of the decedent's children as cotrustees. Every situation is different, which is why there is no one-size-fits-all trust.

After both grantors die or are incapable of acting as trustees, the "successor trustee(s)" takes over as trustee. The successor trustee is not a grantor and cannot change the terms of the trust in most cases but can only carry out the terms of the trust put in place by the grantor (though there are special situations where trust provisions can be changed by a court or a "trust protector," described later).

The trust becomes irrevocable (unchangeable) after the death or disability of the grantors but is revocable (changeable) during their lifetimes so long as they are capable and competent. These are the general rules. However, people often have reasons to do things differently.

For example, one of the two grantors may be the financial manager and the other grantor may not be capable of handling the business decision-making that a trustee needs to be able to do. In that case, the trust may provide that at the death of the financially capable grantor, another person will act as either sole trustee for the surviving grantor or as a cotrustee with the survivor.

Sometimes a couple wants to be certain that a survivor will not be tempted to misuse the trust assets in such a way as to thwart the intentions of the first grantor to die. In that case, a cotrustee may be named along with the survivor just to be certain that trust transactions are being done properly and honestly according to the terms both grantors set up when alive. This method unfortunately can cause friction between the survivor and the cotrustee, because the survivor is no longer solely in charge of her financial affairs. But it is a pretty much guaranteed way of assuring that the trust rules are followed since all trust transactions require two signatures.

Bank trustees typically charge 1 to 1.5 percent of the trust assets annually as a fee for serving as trustee. Family members who are also beneficiaries usually do it for free; however, it is not uncommon to specify a payment to a trustee for carrying out your trust instructions. Trustees are, of course, entitled to any actual expenses they incur, but also may have to take time off work to meet with accountants or real estate agents or to do other trust-related business. Allotting a set amount of money as a trustee fee on top of whatever the trustee may inherit is not at all unusual and is, I think, appropriate. The amount will depend, of course, on the level of work involved. If the trustee is merely going to wrap up your estate, pay the bills, and hand out the money, a lump-sum trustee fee appropriate to the size of the estate would be determined.

However, if the trustee is to continue to act as trustee in years to come to care for the trust fund of a minor or disabled person, an annual fee should be allocated. Keep in mind that a trustee fee is taxable income to the trustee, whereas if you left the trustee a share of the trust as an heir, it would not be considered income, so a share of the estate is more valuable than an equivalent amount of money as a fee. The trust language can make it clear that the larger share is a gift made in gratitude to the person acting as trustee, and not as payment for services.

BACKUP TRUSTEES

What if your selected trustee cannot or will not act as trustee when the time comes? It is always a good idea to have a second and even a third alternate trustee named in your documents.

Just because you have named someone to be your trustee or executor does not mean they are obligated to do it. A few years ago, a woman came to me to represent the estate of her neighbor. The woman had been named by the neighbor as the executor of the will. The estate was not large and the deceased had several children in other states, none of whom liked her. After discussing the probate process with her, I could see she was not happy with the prospect of the big job ahead of her. Finally, I told her she did not have to do it.

She was surprised, having assumed that she had no choice. "Let one of the children be the executor." I said. The will had no backup named, so the children would either have to agree on one or have the judge appoint someone. She left the papers with me and very cheerfully said she would call one of the sons to tell him her decision.

In your trust, there should be language that provides a mechanism for choosing an alternative trustee if there is none named who is able to do the job. I suggest allowing the beneficiaries to elect a trustee if you can't come up with one, with the guardians of child beneficiaries voting for them. There may be other requirements if the trustee will be enforcing restrictions on when and how a beneficiary receives his share of the trust. You cannot have a trustee in charge of his own restrictions, especially in a special-needs trust situation.

WHO CANNOT BE A TRUSTEE

A special-needs trust is a trust set up for a person who is disabled in some way and who relies upon need-based government programs for his support and/or medical care. Qualifying for Medicaid for example, may be extremely important—even vital—to a person with certain needs. Expensive drugs and medical treatment may be far more important to a person than an inheritance, and inheriting something may disqualify that person from those benefits. The reason is that in most cases, a person can only own a certain maximum amount of assets to qualify for the benefits. If he has the ability to control the assets in the trust, the government might say he has the ability to give them all to himself, thereby putting him over the threshold for disqualification. So a discretionary trust is often created to allow a trustee to give the beneficiary certain things to enrich his life but not enough at one time to affect his benefit programs.

Therefore, the beneficiary of a special-needs trust cannot be the sole trustee of that trust. In a special-needs trust, the trustee has the discretionary authority to make whatever distributions the trustee deems appropriate for the beneficiary, provided that benefit programs are not reduced by the distribution. A special-needs beneficiary may end up being disqualified because of the assumed ability to exercise trustee discretion in favor of the beneficiary.

A trustee must be of legal age, must be mentally competent, should be a resident of the United States, and must not be a ward of the state under a guardianship order. It helps if the chosen trustee has a good business head and is well organized. Check with your attorney to see if there are special restrictions in your state. A bond is not normally necessary, but if it is, the trustee has to qualify for the bond. It would usually be required only in a court-ordered guardianship/conservatorship situation.

A bond is a type of insurance policy that covers any losses to the estate due to the misfeasance or malfeasance of the person bonded. Bonds are only given to bondable people—that is, those who have no criminal history or past conduct that would make them a possible risk to the insurance company. So if the conservator of a person's money runs off with it, the bonding company makes good the loss, then goes after the conservator.

COTRUSTEES

I usually recommend cotrustees if possible. The reason is that two or three people acting together are less likely to procrastinate in carrying out the trust instructions and are going to be more likely to keep good records and follow the trust instructions. They watch each other. A trust, being nonsupervised by a court, has no one to report to and no real enforcement mechanism to control the trustee except after the fact. Cotrustees minimize this potential problem.

Here's an example: one of four children is named as trustee. He is supposed to gather all the assets together, pay the bills, sell the real estate, and divide the remaining assets among the four of them. But he is incompetent or, even worse, crooked. So he doesn't tell everyone what he's doing, spends much of the money on himself, and sells things to his friends for less than value, and when he finally pays off the other three, it is only a fraction of what they should have gotten. Okay, he wasn't trustworthy and shouldn't have been named as trustee. What can the others do? They can petition the court to make him account for the missing assets, but if it's gone and he doesn't have anything left, there is no real way to get back what has been wasted. Cotrustees would have avoided that situation.

CHAPTER SEVEN

Making Your Trust Work: Funding

Having a trust is a great thing for many reasons as explained, but one of the main advantages is avoidance of probate. In order to avoid probate, all assets above the probate exemption threshold must either be in the name of the trust at the time of death or pass to the trust at that time by way of beneficiary designation.

In my law practice, it is not unusual to see clients die who had a trust that was not fully "funded" at the time of their death. Funding is just a word to describe the process of transferring assets to the trust. Any assets left out of the trust will have to go through probate to get into the trust. Our goal is to have no assets left out of the trust.

In some cases, there is a trust but no assets at all in the name of the trust—a trust may be fully funded, partially funded, or unfunded. However, we strive for a fully funded trust in order to get the probate-avoidance advantage.

Everything does not have to go to the trust. As stated earlier, the trust only controls the assets it owns or that pass to it at the death of the grantor. Sometimes a grantor will leave a particular asset such as a bank account or insurance policy to a person outside of the trust by way of beneficiary designation or joint ownership. This is often the case in a blended family where one spouse will leave an asset to his separate children, with the balance of all the trust assets going to all of the children of both spouses. The general rule, though, is that all assets should either be in the name of the trust, pass to the trust at death, or pass to someone else at death. Nothing should have to be probated.

FUNDING METHODS

Funding is not particularly difficult for most assets. Here is a list of common assets and how they are typically funded into a trust.

Real Estate

Real estate is transferred to a trust by way of a deed in most cases. The deed is made from the owner of the real estate to the trustee as trustee of the trust. The deed may be deeded from the grantor to the trust as follows: "John Smith as trustee of the John Smith Revocable Trust dated January 2, 2017."

There are two kinds of deeds commonly used. The "warranty deed" is the kind normally provided to the buyer of real estate by the seller. As its name implies, a warranty deed is used to guarantee that the title to the property being sold is genuine and without any encumbrances.

The "quitclaim deed" is most often used by attorneys working with trusts. This deed does not guarantee title to the property but merely says that what is being transferred is all the rights to the property owned by the owner of the property. For transfers into trusts, we do not have to worry about guaranteeing title; we know they own it, so a quitclaim deed works fine and in some jurisdictions is less expensive to file with the county recorder.

In either case, the grantor can either record the deed immediately or deliver it to the trustee to be recorded after the death of the grantor. Attorneys are not in agreement as to whether the deed to the trust should be recorded immediately or later, upon the death of the grantor. The advantage of recording is that the deed cannot be lost and you will know it is in proper recordable form. There are states that say that an unrecorded deed is not valid, cannot be recorded after the death of the grantor, and has not effectively been completed until recording. This is another thing to ask your lawyer.

Recording a deed right away may result in additional paperwork if the grantor decides to sell or refinance the property. There may also be reasons not to record it in scenarios involving bankruptcy or qualification for Medicaid for nursing home or other medical care.

Should you buy other real estate in the future, be sure it is deeded to the trust. Timeshares in vacation property can be put into the trust name. Real estate located in other states may also be put in the name of your trust, thereby avoiding probate in those other states. Property you are buying on a land contract or contract for deed, where you are not given a deed until the property is paid off, is transferred to the trust by way of an assignment form.

Recording a deed makes it public record, which means that anyone who looks can find out that you have a trust. Recording a deed may also affect certain property tax issues such as homestead rights and may result in removing caps on property assessments. Recording fees may also be high in some states. There are often exemptions available for transfers into a person's revocable trust, so be sure to ask the local tax assessor or your attorney.

Also ask your attorney about potential problems with real estate insurance and title insurance if real estate is in the name of the trust.

Bank and Credit Union Accounts

Bank accounts can be put into the name of the trust directly, or, in most institutions, the trust can be named as either a co-owner of an existing account or a beneficiary of the account. The bank may not use the word beneficiary—it may call it a "pay on death" (POD) or "transfer on death" (TOD) designation—but it amounts to the same thing. As trust owners, we do not care how the bank or institution does it, so long as at our deaths the money ends up in the trust without probate.

To accomplish the transfer, you need only take your trust certificate (sometimes called the trust abstract) to the bank, where it will copy the certificate and have you sign the appropriate paperwork to make the transfer. You will find that they have had experience with trusts and will guide you on how they handle these accounts at their bank. They may even use a shortened version of the trust name to fit their system. This is okay.

Other bank-type deposit accounts such as certificates of deposit and money market funds can be handled the same way.

Stocks, Brokerage Accounts

These can also be put directly in the name of the trust, though the transfer process for stocks not being handled by a broker can be trickier. For broker accounts, we send them your trust certificate and they provide the necessary paperwork to either change the account name or put into effect a TOD or POD. This should not be a transaction for which you are charged a fee because it is not a sale or purchase of securities. It is also not a taxable event for capital gains tax purposes.

Stocks that are not being managed in street name or held by your broker are easily identified, since you will have an actual paper stock certificate issued by the corporation and sent to you. Transferring these to your trust requires that you contact the stock office of the corporation and ask for the appropriate paperwork. In most cases, the forms must then be countersigned at your bank or broker with a "medallion signature guarantee," which is something like a fancy notary. After receiving the signed forms and the old certificates, the corporation issues new stock certificates to your trust.

Stock in a "closely held" corporation may only be transferred to your trust if the corporation's bylaws allow it. A closely held corporation is one in which the stock is not publicly traded.

Stock in "subchapter S" corporations may be held in trust but only while the grantor (maker) of the trust is alive. At his death, the trust must distribute the stock to qualified beneficiaries or divest itself of it within a certain period of time, or the corporation risks losing its special tax status.

Online brokerage accounts, such as E-Trade, TD Ameritrade, Scottrade, and others can also be in the name of your trust. In most cases, you can download the forms and instructions from their websites. They will ask that a copy of the trust certificate be sent to them along with the forms, which may have to be notarized.

As for retirement accounts, Keoghs, IRAs, and 401(k)s, be aware that a transfer of such accounts to a living trust may be considered a taxable distribution of deferred income; therefore, *these should not be put in the name of the trust* but should have the trust named as the *contingent beneficiary* of these accounts, with the spouse being the primary beneficiary if that is the case. This is so that upon the death of one spouse, the other retains easier rollover elections. A beneficiary change form and instructions are usually available from the plan administrator.

Government bonds and savings bonds can be transferred to trust ownership through your local bank. The bonds are turned in (not redeemed) to the government, and new bonds are issued in the trust name. Your local bank can provide you with a form PD 1851 to fill out and transfer savings bonds to the name of the trust.

Titled assets such as vehicles, trailers, boats, and motorhomes can be put into trust ownership by having the title changed at the local Secretary of State or state tax office (or whatever the name is for the state agency issuing titles). In some cases this is not necessary. In Michigan, for example, if a person dies who owns a vehicle in her own name and whose will is not going through probate, the "next of kin," typically a spouse or child, can have the title transferred into his or her name directly without any court process merely by presenting the title and death certificate. This process works provided that the total value of the vehicles does not exceed $60,000 or, for boats, $100,000. Relying on this method would not be appropriate for blended families, because whose children get the vehicles depends upon which spouse died last.

Be sure to talk to your accountant about the tax effect of putting a vehicle in the name of your trust and to your insurance agent to be sure the vehicle is still insured if the trust is the owner.

Other Assets and Unusual Situations

Personal property items, such as furniture, collections, clothing, and the contents of your house and garage have no titles so are not individually listed as having been put into the trust. We use a general assignment form to assign all nontitled assets to the trust. Then, if there are specific items you want to go to particular people or organizations, we use a personal property distribution form referenced in the trust document and append it to the trust.

Some assets are difficult or even impossible to put into your trust. Royalties are rights to percentages of profits and can be available for a variety of things. Book royalties will be paid to an author for as long as a book is in publication. Assigning these to a trust will require the permission of the publisher, and I have seen publishers refuse to agree to the assignment. This creates a situation where the estate of the author must deal with royalty checks for years after the rest of the estate has been settled and closed.

Royalties on oil or gas leases are paid for a fixed period of time according to the terms of the original written lease and are typically assignable to a trust. Other royalties on things such as patents, trademarks, copyrights, profit percentages on films, songs, software programs, and business contractual arrangements may or may not be assignable, depending upon the contract that was signed. In my office, we assign these to the trust even if we are not sure, because it costs nothing if we are wrong but is a great advantage if we are right.

Celebrity Images

We have all heard that Elvis and Michael Jackson make more money now than when they were alive. The royalties received by their estates were not assigned to a trust so far as I know, but they could have been. Celebrity images and the use of a name are intangibles that can be assigned to a trust. Otherwise they are payable to the probate estate, sometimes for years.

Animals with pedigree papers can be placed in trust ownership. Registered horses, show dogs, and even cats can be registered in the name of your trust. Animals with no pedigree or "paper" can be made part of the trust assets by using the General Assignment of Assets form, which should be included with every trust. Animals, even your favorite pet dog, are considered personal property by the law, no different from your furniture, and so can be listed in the trust on your "Exhibit A" to specify who should receive them.

Aircraft can be placed directly in trust ownership, provided the FAA rules are followed. These are very complex. An Aircraft Registration Application form (AC 8050-1) must be filled out and submitted with a copy of the trust document and a special affidavit containing specific detailed information. I have had aircraft owners who worked for the FAA tell me that it is nearly impossible to get trust ownership of an aircraft through the bureaucracy. There are a few ways to get around this. A corporation can be created to take ownership of the aircraft and the corporate stock placed in the trust name (using a limited liability company works the same way). Another method is to use joint ownership, presumably with someone younger, to have more than just the original owner's name on the registration.

Contract rights may not be assignable to the trust because the assignment is specifically prohibited. For example, interests in a partnership, a real estate cooperative, or even a small corporation or LLC may have such restrictive provisions. The reasoning is that the co-owners do not want to be stuck with the heirs of the trust grantor as partners after the grantor dies. These types of agreements will have buy-sell agreements or provisions regarding the death of a member if they are well drafted. Often these restrictions were put in place automatically and can be easily changed by your attorney with the consent of the co-owners.

CHAPTER EIGHT

Instructions to You as the Grantor and Trustee

During your lifetime you are the trustee. So you manage and control all trust assets. There is nothing you need to do as trustee that is too different from what you were doing before you had a trust. Operation of your trust is quite simple.

TAXES

There are no separate tax numbers necessary for the trust while you are alive (see Employer Identification Number in the glossary). You file your taxes just as you always have in the past without reference to the trust. There is no trust tax return required unless, at the death of a grantor, the trustee is to take over and continue for the benefit of a trust beneficiary.

BANKING

Once your bank and credit union accounts are either in the name of the trust or have a pay-on-death designation filed for them, you do nothing different from what you did before. Your checks do not have to have the name of the trust imprinted upon them, even though the account is in the name of the trust. You do not have to write the word "trustee" after your signature. See the section on accommodation signatures below if you want to give someone else the permission to use the account on your behalf.

REAL ESTATE

The sale or mortgage of real estate operates in exactly the same fashion as before, except that if the deed to the trust has been recorded, the name of the seller is the trust and you sign as trustee. The buyer or his title company might require an affidavit from you stating that the trust is still in operation and that you have the authority to sell the property. Upon your death, the successor trustee can immediately assign the property of the trust to the heirs as you have instructed (after paying all your debts, taxes, and other expenses, of course). No probate court directives are necessary. The death certificate is normally recorded with the county deeds records.

NEWLY ACQUIRED ASSETS

Don't forget as time goes by that you have a trust. If you buy new real estate, get a deed made to the trust for the new property. Do the same when opening new accounts or acquiring any new titled assets. These must be funded to the trust in order to keep them out of probate. The pour-over will, described previously, will guarantee that these new assets end up in the trust after the pour-over will is probated, but probate avoidance is a major benefit of your trust and it is up to you to see that the trust stays funded.

CHANGING YOUR MIND

Trusts are easily changed. Much more easily, in fact, than wills. To change a will, you need to sign a codicil. This is a written amendment to the will prepared by an attorney that must be signed with the same statutory formality of the will itself, which may mean having two disinterested witnesses and in some cases a notary. Changing a trust in most states can be done merely by signing a dated, written statement explaining what you are changing. In some states, the trust amendment does not even have to be witnessed or notarized, though as a way of avoiding a fight over whether you actually signed the document or whether you were competent when you did it, I recommend having witnesses and notarizing.

The point is that the trust is revocable, which means it is changeable so long as you are mentally competent.

REVOKING THE TRUST

Usually we do not want to revoke the trust since we want the benefits a trust can provide. Amending it for changed circumstances usually works; however, there are situations where you may no longer want the trust.

Death, Divorce, and Remarriage

The joint trust that you had with you ex-spouse will likely have to be revoked and redone as an individual trust. The reason is that you were both probably named as cotrustees during your lifetime and each other's trustee upon death or disability. The distribution plans of each of your assets are likely different than when you were married. The old trust must be "defunded" and the assets placed either in your individual names or the names of your new individual trusts. Don't forget to change beneficiary designations on accounts to the new trust name.

Defunding just means taking the assets out of the trust name. While you can sign a document that says the old trust is officially revoked, that is not necessary unless the trust is registered with a court. The trust ceases to exist for all intents and purposes when it has nothing left in its name and nothing is to pass to it on anyone's death.

If you were single when you made the trust and are now married, you will want to talk to your lawyer about how this affects the trust. In community property states (most of the western states plus Wisconsin), you may have to either make a new trust or have your new spouse sign off on your trust plan. A spouse may automatically accede to rights in your trust property by virtue of the marriage. In any event, you will probably want to amend the trust to provide for the new wife or husband. Typical provisions may include use or ownership of the marital home if you die first.

Trust Purpose Is Gone

A trust set up for a particular purpose, such as a special-needs trust or an educational or spendthrift trust, has a certain life expectancy. When the trust purpose has been fulfilled, the terms of the trust determine the disposition of the remaining trust assets. When that happens, the trust expires. There are no papers to file or forms to fill out. There may be a final trust tax return, but that's it.

It may be that you lived longer than expected or some other circumstance caused you to use up your assets to the point where your estate at death falls below the probate threshold. In that case, you may just remove all assets from the trust. There is no need to cancel the trust, and there are no forms you need to file. It just sits there empty until you either die or add assets to it.

In the event of a trust that is being supervised by a court, you will have to file a petition to close the trust and may have to have the approval of the court. Discuss this with your attorney if that comes up. I see few of these, but it could happen.

CHAPTER NINE

You Do Not Need a Trust If . . .

I know I stated earlier that nearly everyone needs a trust for one reason or another, but in certain very limited situations, a trust may not be needed for some people. Sometimes cost is a concern, as having an attorney prepare a trust can cost much more than will preparation and you may just not be able to afford the trust.

ALTERNATIVES TO WILLS AND TRUSTS

I typically prepare a handful of wills each year and hundreds of trusts. Sometimes I send potential clients away with neither. Below are some examples of reasons why.

No Probatable Assets

A person who owns no real estate or investments often will not go through probate, so probate avoidance would not be a reason to have a trust. Bank accounts can have co-owners on them or, in some cases, beneficiaries (sometimes called pay-on-death designees). If a person wants his limited assets to be given to particular people with no strings attached, assuming the people to whom the assets are to be given are adults not suffering from any disability, a beneficiary designation or co-owner on the account may be all he needs to meet his estate planning needs. (Even those who do not need a trust should still have a durable power of attorney and medical directive—more on this in chapter 11).

Small estates will not have to be probated. In most states, there is a threshold below which estates do not have to go through the whole probate process. Usually there is a simplified way to transfer small-sized estates to the beneficiaries. It may be by use of a notarized affidavit or by use of short forms filed with the appropriate court office.

The threshold varies from state to state. In California, for instance, estates under $100,000 do not have to go through probate. In Michigan, the amount is much lower, based on a formula that amounts to $20,000 after the deduction of funeral and burial expenses. There are also other deductions that can be made in specific circumstances—usually for married couples or those with minor children to increase the threshold amount. These may be called spousal allowances, homestead allowances, or exempt property, but the idea is that you may not have to go through full-blown probate, depending upon the nature and amount of the assets of the deceased.

Beneficiary Designations

Beneficiary designations can be a way of avoiding probate if there are no other probatable assets. Probatable assets are those that must go through the probate process in order to transfer the title to the heirs who are supposed to receive them. Some assets, though, are not subject to probate, because there is another way of transferring them. Joint ownership, described in the next section, is one way, and beneficiary designations are another. Keep in mind that a personal trust may be designated as a beneficiary of an account as described in chapter 7.

Examples of assets that may be transferred by way of a beneficiary designation follow.

Life Insurance. Everyone knows that life insurance is left to the policy owner's survivors by way of a written beneficiary designation. The beneficiary then is the person who receives the life insurance payoff at the insured's death. Suppose there is no named beneficiary who survives the insured. In most cases, the "estate" of the insured receives the death benefit.

"Estate of the insured" refers to the probate estate of the insured. So probate is necessary in this case to cash the check for the life insurance, provided that it exceeds the probate threshold in the state of residence of the deceased.

Insurance policy provisions can change this result by setting up default beneficiaries in the event a beneficiary dies. For example, the policy may provide that the money goes to the insured's next of kin. Talk to the lawyer.

If the deceased had a trust, then the trust would be named as the beneficiary. If not, then individuals would be named to get the death benefits. It is possible to leave beneficiaries different shares of a life insurance policy. For example, you may say your son is to get 40 percent of the life insurance as a beneficiary and your daughter to receive 60 percent. Beneficiaries do not have to be treated equally.

Retirement Accounts. Tax-deferred accounts come in many flavors, such as IRAs, 401(k)s, 403(b)s, SEP accounts, tax-deferred annuities, and many more. All of these can be left to an heir by naming that person as the beneficiary of the account. The beneficiary then steps into your shoes in a way, since he has the ability most of the time to make his own elections as to when and how much to withdraw from the account.

Joint Ownership. One of the traditional ways of avoiding probate, often recommended by lawyers, was to add someone's name on an account or a parcel of real estate. At the death of the original owner, all that had to be shown was the death certificate, and the property belonged to the survivor. It does work to avoid probate. Unfortunately, joint ownership, if not set up correctly, can lead to unanticipated problems. For example, putting someone else's name on your property can mean that you now need the co-owner's permission (and in some states if he is married, his wife's) to mortgage or sell the property. If he refuses, there may be nothing you can do about it. So be cautious using this approach. It can also lead to loss of the "stepped-up tax basis" causing the new owner expensive capital gains taxes at the time of your death. Merely putting the property in a trust or in a special type of joint deed (such as the ladybird deed explained later in this chapter) gives you the stepped-up tax basis at death and minimizes any capital gains tax.

Gifts. Putting someone else's name on your account or property with the intention that they receive it at your death is a gift to them. The gift is subject to federal gift tax laws, and if the value of the gift exceeds the annual exclusion amount ($14,000 at the time of this writing), a gift tax return is supposed to be filed to give that information to the IRS. The annual exclusion amount applies to each person to whom you give a gift. No gift tax is due unless the total value of all gifts in excess of the annual exclusions is greater than $5.45 million during your lifetime.

Also, the making of the gift means that the assets are now assets of the new owner and subject to the claims of the new owner's creditors, including being reachable in bankruptcy proceedings, and may become marital property for divorce property division purposes. Do you want your property tied up in this manner? Probably not, which is why a trust is the best way to handle your estate plan.

Tax Basis

The whole area of tax basis, carryover tax basis, and stepped-up tax basis is in flux right now. Under current law, making a gift of property to a person by putting his name on it as a way of avoiding probate may result in a much lower tax basis for that person (meaning higher capital gains taxes) than would putting it into a trust where he could elect to get a stepped-up tax basis (meaning lower capital gains taxes).

Loss of Control

Once you put someone's name on your real estate, you now need his permission (and the permission of the wife of a male co-owner in most states) to sell, mortgage, or give away the property. Most people do not want to give up the control of their own real estate. I once had a two-year court battle representing a mother who wanted to get her children's names off her deeds—something she did on the advice of her not-so-smart attorney.

Probate Not Avoided

Probate is not avoided; it is merely postponed. While probate is avoided on the death of one person, at the death of the survivor, the property would have to be probated to go to the heirs of the survivor. The survivor would need to make his or her own estate plan to cover this problem.

Transfer on Death Deeds (Ladybird Deeds)

There are many people who have very little in assets other than their home and a very simple plan for those assets at death. A full-blown trust-based estate plan may be too expensive for them. In those situations, there is a simple alternative. It does involve a type of joint deed, which I have just warned about, but by setting it up properly, you can avoid most of the pitfalls of joint deeds and still avoid probate. This type of deed is sometimes called a "ladybird deed" after the former first lady, wife of President Lyndon B. Johnson, part of whose estate was handled in this manner.

The deed says that the grantor of the property is adding one or more names to the deed, but until the grantor's death, she still retains the right to sell, mortgage, or transfer the property without the permission of the new co-owners. In effect, a gift is made, but it is a contingent gift (what lawyers call a gift of a future interest), which may or may not come to fruition. If the grantor sells the property, the interests of the newly added people are revoked. Because the gift is contingent, the new people cannot exercise any rights of ownership, the property is not reachable by their creditors, and the grantor does not need their permission to mortgage or sell the property. It becomes like a mini-trust.

Some attorneys are now drafting the ladybird deed even for people with regular trusts, naming the trust as the contingent joint owner in answer to some court decisions that put into question the availability of title insurance for trust property or of Medicaid qualification. Medicaid is the federal program providing medical care for indigents. It is administered by the states, and each state has its own requirements for qualifying for this benefit. The common requirements are meeting certain minimum asset and income limitations. So a person who does not qualify because she exceeds the asset threshold may be able to change the ownership status of some of the assets to fit into the program.

The rest of the assets of the grantor should either be handled with beneficiary or transfer-on-death provisions; if they are small enough in value to fall below the threshold for requiring formal probate in that state, they may qualify for an expedited or affidavit probate process.

The grantor still should have a durable power of attorney, medical power of attorney, and living will, as explained in chapter 12.

CHAPTER TEN

The Many Types of Trusts

"Trust" is only five letters long, but it is a big word. The first distinction, as alluded to earlier, is that between a trust contained in a will, a testamentary trust, and a stand-alone document, which may be either a revocable trust or an irrevocable trust. We are talking about the nontestamentary, nonprobatable trusts.

There are dozens of kinds of trusts, complex and simple, for all sorts of purposes. In this book, we are talking about fairly simple trusts, which the IRS refers to as "revocable grantor trusts" (what we normally call revocable living trusts). Revocable just means changeable. The grantor is the person who owns the trust itself. Sometimes they call the grantor the settlor, but it's the same thing. During the grantor's lifetime, he may change or revoke the trust. At his death or disability, the trust is unchangeable or irrevocable. I am not going to go into detail describing the many trusts available for many different purposes, since this would go beyond my intentions for this book.

Other trusts may be created for avoidance or minimization of estate taxes. There are a lot of kinds of trusts for those purposes, which can be complex and require the services of a skilled tax or estate planning attorney. Listing and defining all the variations of these trusts goes beyond the scope and intent of this book. The trusts needed by 95 percent of us are for the following purposes.

Probate avoidance is a common benefit shared by all the trusts we use. While probate does not have to be expensive or time-consuming, in many instances it is just that. As I have stated previously, there is no advantage whatsoever to anyone to have your estate go through probate. The only exception, of course, is the probate attorney, who receives a big fee for handling the estate. With a properly funded trust, there should be no need for court or even attorney involvement in your estate after your death.

Management of assets for beneficiaries is an extremely good reason to have a trust, and this type of trust is essential for anyone with minor children, disabled beneficiaries who are dependent upon federal or state aid, or spendthrifts who cannot manage their own money effectively. Without this type of asset-management trust, the money being inherited would go in a lump sum to the beneficiary, which might cause disastrous consequences.

As discussed in chapter 2, a lump-sum distribution to a child when he reaches adulthood is usually a bad idea. Most parents want their children to have the benefit of their inheritance but would prefer to have someone else assist in managing that money to be sure that it is put to the most beneficial use and is not wasted.

Having the money held in trust for the child solves that potential problem. The trust itself is not "funded" until the death of the grantor. At that time the trustee begins managing the money for the beneficiary and follows the trust instructions as to when to make trust distributions, for what purposes, and in what amounts. The rules set up for distributions are varied. Common examples of how people do it are:

Attaining a certain age. All the money is held in trust until the beneficiary reaches age twenty-five, for example. Up until then the trustee may be given the authority to use the money for the beneficiary's health, education, welfare, and general living expenses. I have even seen people set up requirements that a portion of the money is to be held as a retirement account for the beneficiary to be turned over to him at age sixty-two and invested until then, essentially creating a retirement account for someone who might otherwise not have one. There may even be provisions allowing money to be paid out in certain limited instances such as medical emergencies. There also must be a provision saying where the money goes if the beneficiary dies before age sixty-two.

A variation on this is giving installments upon the beneficiary attaining different age levels, such as one-third at twenty-five, one-half the balance at thirty, and the remaining balance at thirty-five to split the inheritance into shares so that if a mistake is made with one installment, the beneficiary gets two more shots at it. People often want to split up the inheritance no matter the age of the beneficiary—perhaps one-third at the time of death of grantor, one-half the balance five years later, and the remaining balance ten years after the death of the grantor.

Attaining certain benchmarks. The trust may provide no money to be distributed until the beneficiary does certain things, such as graduating from college, acting as a missionary for a time, or getting married. There should be a default provision that would say where the money goes if the benchmark is not achieved. One example would be that the person would then have to wait until reaching age fifty.

JOINT OR INDIVIDUAL TRUSTS FOR COUPLES

Couples can do their estate planning together by having a joint trust, or they may each have their own trust. Which is best depends upon the intentions of the couple, the nature of their assets, and the size of the total asset mix.

For the traditional family unit with a husband, wife, and children (who are the children of both parents) who do not have enough assets to worry about estate taxes (under $5.45 million) and who agree on a plan of asset distribution at both their deaths, a simple joint marital trust is the best answer. Only one-fifth of 1 percent of Americans have enough assets at death to pay estate taxes. That is not many, and those folks are not the focus of this book. They need more complex tax-planning advice, though they still need some sort of trust. (Keep in mind that even if the federal estate tax is eliminated entirely, as is proposed, state inheritance taxes may be reinstated. The law in this are is frequently changed.)

Joint trusts can be made for married couples, gay and other unmarried couples, and even a parent and child. Any two or more people can make a joint trust. Funding a joint trust is easy, since all the grantors put their assets into one trust name—for example, "The John Smith and Mary Doe Revocable Trust." Typical provisions allow both of them to be trustees, and when one dies, the survivor continues on in control of all the trust assets without restriction on the ability to use the trust assets and may still have the full right to change the trust terms in any way the survivor desires.

But restrictions can be put into the trust language. For example, there may be a requirement that a survivor cannot change the trust terms in such a way as to disinherit the family of the first trust grantor to die—sort of an anti-disinheritance clause. The terms of the trust may also have different results as to distribution of trust assets, depending upon who is the last to die. So if John were the survivor, the assets would be split one way, and if Mary were the survivor, they would be split differently.

Often the two grantors will agree on appointing co-successor trustees—one from his side of the family and one from hers.

Individual trusts are most often used for single people who are not in a joint relationship, but not always, as I will explain. The one-person trust has one grantor, and all assets are funded into the name of that trust. The grantor retains all authority over the trust and its assets and controls who gets what and when after he dies.

Married couples often have individual trusts primarily for tax purposes, but also for spousal and family protection.

The traditional estate planning method attorneys have used for married couples with an estate that is potentially subject to estate tax is the so-called "A/B trust." This is really two trusts—a husband trust and a wife trust. The couple's assets are split, with a portion going to one and the rest to the other. At the death of one of the spouses the trust of the deceased is then divided into two portions, an A trust and a B trust. To avoid confusion, we will call the A trust the family trust and the B trust the marital trust.

The survivor usually has some significant restrictions on the use of the assets in the deceased partner's family trust. The income from the family trust is payable to the survivor along with up to 5 percent or $5,000 per year of the principal, whichever is greater. Other than that, the principal itself may not be invaded unless the assets in the survivor's trust are insufficient to maintain the survivor's normal and accustomed standard of living.

At the death of the survivor, both trusts would be distributed to the ultimate beneficiaries named in the trusts. The advantage of this rather cumbersome arrangement is a doubling of the estate tax exemption to avoid estate tax. This is a very necessary objective when the estate tax exemption is low. Estate taxes are charged on the value of an estate that exceeds a minimum threshold. Right now, that amount is quite high at $5.45 million and is supposed to be permanent, but seems to change with each president. So for most of us, estate taxes are not a concern.

We still sometimes use this method for large estates, although I refer these to tax experts for planning.

There is a simpler way that utilizes a joint trust to accomplish the same thing. What I call the joint option trust allows all the advantages of the simple joint trust but retains the tax advantages if necessary. This is a good option for couples who agree on an ultimate plan of distribution and who will be the successor trustee. The language of this trust states that at the death of one grantor, the survivor determines whether the current asset size of the joint estate is more than the current estate tax exemption amount. If it is not, the survivor needs to do nothing and has no restrictions on the use of all the trust assets from then on. If it is more, the survivor then allocates the excess taxable portion to a family trust and the balance goes to the marital trust. As we know, there are no restrictions on the marital trust, so this is a great advantage to a surviving grantor.

Single trusts are used by married couples for other reasons. Let's say the wife has a lot of assets that were brought into the marriage and wants to be sure that her husband is cared for during his lifetime. However, she also wants to be sure that at the death of her husband the remaining assets go to her children. She can create a single trust funded with her assets that contains these provisions. She and her husband may also create a separate joint trust for their other assets, and he may have a single trust of his own with similar provisions to hers.

Other kinds of trusts include such things as educational trusts for children, land trusts, and various kinds of charitable trusts, which provide income to the grantor for life with the trust going to the charity at death. There are many others, which I did not cover because the focus of this book is on trusts for the majority of people who are not likely to need tax planning or complex estate plans. Other tax issues such as stepped-up tax basis for capital gains assets are in the venue of your tax advisor or attorney.

CHAPTER ELEVEN

Problems with Trusts

Trusts are not a panacea. That is, there can be problems associated with using a trust as an estate settlement method. Trust is the primary problem. Your trustee has to be trustworthy. Since there is no oversight by a court or anyone else, the trustee is the one responsible for making good decisions—investment decisions, financial management decisions, and so forth.

For example, in a down stock market it may be wise to hold stocks for a period of time rather than selling to protect the value of the trust principal. Timing of the sale of assets is a financial management decision. Selecting which assets in which to invest trust funds is a critical decision. Trustees are supposed to be conservative and, absent instructions to the contrary, are supposed to diversify the trust investments. Certainly we would not want to choose a trustee who might invest all the funds in a risky stock.

But because there is no oversight, the only ones the trustee has to report to are the trust beneficiaries, and then only after the fact. The trustee is required to keep good records and keep the trust beneficiaries informed as to trust income and expenses. Unfortunately, by the time the beneficiaries find out about a mistake, the money may already be gone with no way to recover it.

How do we remedy this potential problem? There are four ways:

1. Find a very reliable trustee who will not make these mistakes and who will act honestly. This is a judgment call at best. Most of the time trustees *do* act honestly and competently and there are no problems. Do not take the warnings here as any indication that trustee abuse is widespread, because it is actually quite rare.
2. Use cotrustees. When more than one trustee is responsible for trust management, there is less likelihood of sloppy bookkeeping, poor asset management, or a trustee embezzling the trust funds.
3. Use an institutional trustee. Banks and trust companies are in the business of acting as trustees and managing trust funds. Their fees typically are about 1 percent of the trust assets per year, but they often can make that up in higher earnings than an individual trustee investor can achieve.
4. Register the trust with the court. Most courts have procedures that allow a trust to be supervised by the local probate court. While this may be more trouble for the trustee and may incur annual attorney fees, it is a way of insuring as best we can that the trust instructions will be carried out and that the trust assets will be preserved. Generally, we do not want court oversight because of the additional paperwork and bureaucracy attendant, but if you are unsure of your trustee's likelihood of acting in the best interests of your estate, you may want to go for it.
5. Give all trust beneficiaries a copy of the trust and a let them know about the responsibilities of the named

trustee. The beneficiaries need to be educated as to what a trust is and their rights and responsibilities. One big problem is that lack of communication may cause each beneficiary to hire a separate attorney, which really stirs up the mud and complicates things. (You could also give them each a copy of this book.)

THE TRUST PROTECTOR

The Uniform Trust Act, which is currently in force or pending in a couple dozen states, provides potential protection for trust beneficiaries from a wayward trustee or from changes in circumstance. The act allows the grantors of the trust to appoint a third party or a committee of outside people to supervise the trustee.

The protector's role is set out in the language of the trust document. The protector may be given limited rights to be sure that the intent of the grantor(s) is carried out. These powers may include the right to change the trustee, to change the terms of the trust, or even to add beneficiaries under certain conditions. The rights of the protector are limited to what is given to him in the trust. The purpose is first to be sure the trustee is doing what is supposed to be done. The second purpose is to be sure that if unexpected changes occur, the trust is still going to do what was intended. For example, the trust may provide for a share of the trust assets to be given to the five grandchildren of the grantors. Perhaps at the time the trust was made there was no likelihood that there would be any more grandchildren. Then—surprise—another one is born. The protector may be given the ability to add the new grandchild as a beneficiary even if the grantors are long dead.

Or maybe the trustee is just not doing the job properly. Rather than having to go through the probate court to have the trustee replaced, the protector could be given the right to have the trustee replaced. This saves time and money for the beneficiaries.

Or there may be a change in the tax laws that would benefit the trust estate if the trust language could be changed. The protector could do that.

Family members and beneficiaries should not be the protector, though they may be considered as a committee the protector consults before making a change in the trust. Typically, the protector would be the family accountant, a trusted financial advisor, or another disinterested, nonbeneficiary third party.

This is not a role that should be put in every trust. In most cases, the trust provisions provide for a complete distribution of trust assets soon after death. In continuing trusts, though, a protector may be advantageous to cover the ongoing events and life changes that may present themselves. Also, keep in mind that you are adding another layer of complexity to the trust process by having a protector, and that this is a paying position. A protector could be a pricey position to create if it is not strictly needed.

Actually, it is not necessary for the Uniform Trust Act to be enacted in your state for you to have a protector. Trusts are so flexible that you can add the specific language to create this position even without the act. Just be careful putting it in if it is not needed, since this means there is someone looking over the shoulder of the trustee at all times and may add significant cost and delay to the trust settlement process.

TRUSTS AND CREDITORS

A revocable trust does not provide asset protection. There are seminars and courses offered that promote the use of trusts as a way of protecting your assets from your creditors. Most of these involve the use of either irrevocable trusts or offshore trusts with foreign trustees and are sold for big prices by those running the seminars. In some cases these techniques work, but sometimes they can be disastrous, and the trust owner finds himself prosecuted for fraudulent transfers or income tax evasion. Be very careful and get independent legal advice before using any of these types of trusts. Similarly, having your assets in a revocable trust does not guarantee that you will qualify for Medicaid benefits for nursing-home care. The asset and income limitations still apply, and trust assets are considered as your assets for qualification purposes.

The purpose of the revocable living trust is not creditor protection. The trust described in this book has as its purposes—probate avoidance, asset management, and estate tax minimization—but not protection from creditors or lawsuits.

GUARDIAN AND TRUSTEE ARE TWO DIFFERENT ROLES

One problem we occasionally see is when the guardian of minor children is also named as the trustee of their trust-fund money. This is an inherent conflict of interest, because the guardian would be the one asking the trustee for funds for the care of the children. It sounds okay but can lead to abuses.

Here's an example: Mom and Dad died, leaving three young children as survivors. A friend of the family was named as their trustee and guardian. The trustee had children of her own and made a decision to use the trust funds to add onto her house to provide a playroom for all the children. While this decision temporarily benefited the children, in the long run it benefited the trustee, because the money added to the value of her home. (She had to give the money back.)

Had the trustee and guardian roles been separated, it is unlikely the trustee would have agreed to the building of the playroom.

WHY YOU MAY NOT WANT A JOINT TRUST

A joint trust between two or more people normally will have their joint and individual assets funded into it. Then there is one set of instructions that tells the trustee what to do with those assets at one or both deaths. The first thing that is done after identifying the assets is paying the debts. That can be a problem.

If one partner has a lot of debt that is not jointly owed by the other partner, the amount of the individual debt will have to be paid from the joint trust assets at the death of the debtor. This can be disastrous to the surviving grantor.

I had a client whose husband, who was seriously ill, owed over $100,000 resulting from a lawsuit over a failed business venture. At his death, the joint trust would have been responsible for the entire debt, even though most of the assets belonged to the wife before the marriage. Fortunately, before he died, we were able to revoke the joint trust, remove her assets, and set up an individual trust for her. When he died, only his separate assets were liable for the debt, so the wife's assets were preserved. Analyze the respective debts of the two grantors to see if this could be an issue.

CHAPTER TWELVE

Guardians, Powers of Attorney, and Other Documents

The trust document creates your trust and says who gets what and when as well as who sees to it that your wishes are followed. But it is only one of several documents that together make up your estate plan.

GUARDIANSHIP OF CHILDREN

All states allow a parent to nominate the guardian who will take over the raising of children at the death of the parents. If you are divorced, the surviving parent will typically become the custodian automatically, but we recommend naming a guardian anyway, just in case the other parent is unable or unwilling to act as guardian.

The guardian is the person who takes the place of the parent in raising the child. This person will also be the Social Security payee for survivor's benefits. The conservator is the person who handles the child's money that may not be part of the child's trust funds and is supervised by the courts.

Naming a guardian is typically done by language in a will, though in some states it can also be done by affidavit. The statement is simple, merely stating something like this: "I nominate and appoint Mary Doe of 123 Maple Street, Detroit, Michigan, as guardian of my minor children." Nothing fancy or complicated but legally sufficient when signed and witnessed in a properly drafted will.

Usually we name the person as "conservator" of the children's money as well, though if the guardian is not the trustee of the children's money, we would name the trustee as the conservator.

But isn't the point of this book to use trusts and not wills? Yes. However, in every trust-based estate plan, there is still a will, though it is rarely used to transfer assets and is usually not probated because the trust takes care of all that. The will does have another use.

The will is one way to name a guardian and conservator for your children even if it is not formally probated. Your trust-based estate plan containing a pour-over will takes care of naming guardians for your minor children.

GUARDIANSHIP OF ADULTS

There is a whole section of the court system devoted to adult guardianship. Adults have accidents and strokes, develop Alzheimer's disease and dementia, or have physical conditions that render them unable to care for themselves. If proper planning has not been done, the person's family is forced to petition the court for guardianship and conservatorship in order to care for the person.

Court-supervised guardianship and conservatorship is a burdensome problem for the family. While the purpose is to be sure that the person and his finances are properly cared for, the court oversight and reporting requirements are a lot to put family members through. The court hearings, which are periodically required, may take most of a day and typically involve just waiting for your turn in front of the judge. Attorney fees are often required, as are court costs and a court-appointed guardian ad litem (a court-appointed person who is watching out for the interests of the person who needs the guardianship, usually an attorney), who charges the estate as well.

To avoid the court-ordered adult guardianship, all you have to have are two documents in addition to the trust itself. These are part of every well-drawn estate plan.

Durable Power of Attorney

A durable power of attorney is a permission slip entitling someone else to legally sign your name. It gives them the right to sign documents with the same authority and legal effect as if you had signed them yourself. Deeds, checks, tax returns, and any other document that you authorize can be signed by the person who has your power of attorney, who is, in effect, your agent. Thus, your agent can pay your bills for you and do your business without getting permission from the courts. (Lawyers sometimes call your agent your "attorney-in-fact" even though these agents are not necessarily attorneys.)

There are two basic kinds of powers of attorney: immediate and springing. An immediate power of attorney is effective, valid, and usable the moment it is signed. We use this for those who want someone to help them pay their bills and manage things for them because they need the help right now. Maybe they can do it themselves, but it is more convenient to have someone's help. A son or daughter may run to the bank for an elderly parent who has physical limitations, for example, even though mentally the parent has no diminished capacity.

A springing power of attorney only goes into effect if a certain condition is met. Typically this might be if two physicians certify in writing that the person is incapable, due to physical or mental incapacity, of making reasoned decisions regarding his financial affairs. This is the kind most younger people want since they are healthy and do not want someone else to have the broad authority over their accounts and assets.

The danger of a power of attorney is that it can be misused. Since the agent can sign your name, she can do anything you can do, including sell your real estate, empty your bank accounts, and even borrow money on your credit. Be very careful to whom you give this power.

A power of attorney may be limited as to time or may be limited in scope. It may be convenient to have someone sit in for you on a real estate closing while you attend to other business. That person can sign all the necessary paperwork and receive the sale proceeds with a power of attorney. This type of document could be written to specifically limit the power of attorney to that one transaction, for a limited time period, and then the power of attorney would automatically expire.

In the estate planning area, we typically use very broad powers of attorney. The only restriction is that the agent, in most cases, cannot create or modify a person's will or trust.

A power of attorney can be revoked at any time by the maker by notifying the agent in writing. If this happens, it is a good idea to also contact any financial institutions that the agent may have dealt with to let them know of the revocation of authority and supply them with a new document containing the new agent's name.

One caveat: sometimes powers of attorney will not be honored even if properly drawn up. While these are legal documents, there is no law at this time in most states that requires a financial institution or anyone else to recognize the authority of the agent. Not honoring powers of attorney is rare, but it does happen and there is no way to force the issue. Legislation has been drafted to overcome this problem, but in most states the problem exists. It is not a bad idea to have your power of attorney redone more often as you get older even if there are no changes. Institutions prefer more recent powers of attorney, and some will not honor those more than a year old.

Medical Power of Attorney

This is the second document needed to protect against court-ordered adult guardianship. Similar to the durable general power of attorney, the medical power of attorney grants to some other person the right to make medical decisions for you if you cannot make them for yourself. This decision-making authority is for such things as consenting to surgery and medical procedures but also extends to decisions on termination or continuation of life support, so picking the person with this power is a serious decision. You should also consider whether the person you are naming is emotionally capable of acting in this capacity. Terminating life support is a heavy burden, and some people just cannot do it, even if that is what the patient wants.

If you have a revocable trust, a durable power of attorney, and a medical power of attorney, it is unlikely that a judge would bother appointing a guardian or conservator, since you have all the help you need in the event of disability. Some of the petitions to appoint a guardian and conservator—the court-promulgated documents—even ask the question of whether such documents already exist.

DEFINING DISABILITY

Disagreements over when a person is actually mentally disabled to the extent that he or she can no longer make reasoned and intelligent decisions regarding legal or financial matters are common. Often children will disagree as to the extent of a parent's disability. The parent herself my feel she is perfectly capable of continuing to run her own affairs, but the kids don't think so. These situations lead to family disharmony and often end up being fought out in court. A potentially embarrassing event for the alleged incapacitated, as she is sitting there while the doctors and children testify as to all the things going wrong. And competency hearings are always expensive, sometimes involving multiple attorneys.

This catastrophe can be easily avoided by proper language in the trust and power of attorney defining how to determine incapacity. You, as the trust owner are telling your heirs that if certain conditions are met, then you voluntarily relinquish control and let your trustees take over.

The conditions are up to you. Here are some ideas. The beauty of using these instructions is that you are the one who decides when incapacity exists. Remember though that a court can always overrule you. We do the best we can to convince them otherwise.

Let the children decide. This option puts a lot of faith in your children that they will do what is in your best interests, not their own. You could state in writing that if the majority of children (or all if you like) agree in writing that you are no longer capable of managing your legal and financial affairs due to mental or physical incapacity, they agree to empower your named trustee (s) to take over. The potential problem with this option is that you may not agree that you are incapable. You would then be in the awkward position of having to try to amend your documents to change that provision and may have to go to court to do so. However, in a tightly knit family where there is harmony and consensus, this may be a good option for you.

Get a medical professional's opinion. State for example that if two licensed psychiatric or medical professionals agree in a written statement that it is their opinion that you are incapable of handling your legal and financial affairs due to mental or physical incapacity, then your trustee may attach those statements to your trust and springing power of attorney and that the successor trustee and attorney-in-fact are now in control of your affairs.

A third option would be you voluntarily agreeing that if a court-ordered guardian and conservator is required, that you want those persons to be the same as you named as your trustee, attorney-in-fact, and medical decision-maker. This would help ensure that someone you do not want acting for you would not be automatically considered for those roles, or worse, that an unknown person, such as a court-appointed attorney charging big fees would not be appointed. A judge can do whatever she wants within reason, but most will want to follow your wishes.

You can of course go ahead and nominate someone to act for you at any time if you think the time has come to let go of the reigns. The potential issue would be whether you were competent when you made that change or if you were being influenced by someone to do something you normally wouldn't do. Undue influence, if proven, could void your choice. It is a good idea to have a video made of you stating your decision with the reasons why and then have your attorney draw up the paperwork after a private conference with you. The attorney would then be a good witness, if it came to that, as to your competency.

I have had several instances where I was able to forestall an undue influence situation. In one case, a man brought his older "friend" to my office and told me that the man wanted to make a will and leave everything to him. I explained I would have to talk to the older gentleman in private due to attorney confidentiality (not necessarily true, but I suspected what was going on). When I talked to the man, it was clear to me he did not understand what was happening, and he said he didn't know who the guy was that brought him there. I refused to do anything and contacted the Adult Protective Services office after they left. I am quite sure though that they went down the block to the next attorney's office and eventually found someone to make a will. (My hope is that when my children come for my car keys, the self-driving car will be ubiquitous and I can drive off somewhere.)

LIVING WILL

If someone is going to make medical decisions for you, he or she will want to know what decisions to make. The living will (which is not a will at all) is a document you sign in which you state your wishes as to the use of life support, feeding tubes, organ donation, medical procedures, and such. While not a legally binding document in most states, it is a good thing to have because it avoids any disagreement among family members as to what you want done in particular situations if you are unable to tell them yourself.

PERSONAL PROPERTY DESIGNATIONS

In a good trust, there will be an addendum (which is just a blank page at the end of your trust, sometimes called Exhibit A) on which you can list particular items of personal property and who is to get each item. You do not have to use the form, but if there are special one-of-a-kind items like wedding rings or Grandpa's shotgun, having a signed statement by you as to who is supposed to get those items avoids a lot of misunderstanding among the family. These provisions can be written into the trust document itself, but if you want to make a minor change, you would need to go back to the attorney to have an amendment done. With the addendum, you just write what the item is and who gets it in your own handwriting. So when you buy that new snow blower, you can write in that it goes to your youngest daughter or whomever. Easy.

TRUST CERTIFICATE

This is a document containing a summary of certain parts of your trust language. It may also be called a certificate of trust existence, an abstract of trust, or another title, but the purpose is the same. It is requested by institutions to prove that the trustee has the authority, and the trust has the power, to conduct certain transactions. It may be used by a real estate title insurance company to guarantee that real estate being sold or mortgaged in the trust name is legally sufficient, title-wise. Brokers and bankers may want a copy as evidence of the existence of the trust, its proper name and date, and identification of the trustees and successor trustees. At your death, when your successor trustee shows up at the bank with your death certificate, the banker will know from the trust documents that he is turning over your accounts to the correct person. If you should change successor trustees, be sure to replace the trust certificates at these institutions to reflect the correct names.

Unfortunately, title companies and banks will not accept the original trust certificate made when you created your trust if it is more than 30 days old. They will want a new document and sometimes may even want a copy of the entire trust. They do not need to see your entire trust. The only part they need is the sections naming the trustees and what powers the trustees have relating to transferring assets such as real estate, stock, or deposit accounts. I suggest asking them for a form that would have language acceptable to them and copy that, attaching a photocopy of the relevant portions of your trust. Or have your attorney prepare a trust certificate for you. It shouldn't cost too much.

CHAPTER THIRTEEN

Trustee Instructions for Death or Disability of the Trust Owner

So now we know why a trust is necessary, what kind of trust to get, how to get it prepared, and how to fund it. But what happens next? What happens to the trust when the trust owner becomes disabled or dies? Most of the information we see about trusts from seminars, news articles, and books explains why a trust is needed and how to go about funding one. There is very little information out there on what to do with the trust at the death of the trust owner.

DISABILITY

One of the reasons we recommend a trust over a will is that the trust can provide an automatic manager of the trust assets if the grantor becomes disabled. People with dementia or who have had strokes or other disabilities may not be able to take care of their financial or legal affairs. Someone has to be able to pay the bills, do the taxes, and manage the money. Without a trust, the family would be forced to petition the probate court for the power to take over. As discussed earlier, this is a time-consuming and expensive process. Part of this can be done with power of attorney, but the rules of the trust itself give the second-in-line trustee—the successor trustee—the power to take over, should this situation occur.

Typically, the successor trustee would meet with the grantor's doctor and, if appropriate, the social worker at the hospital or nursing home to be sure there is a confirmed diagnosis of disability. A written opinion of the diagnosis is best. This satisfies the trust language, which requires proof of actual disability. Armed with this and the power of attorney, the successor trustee can then contact bankers and investment advisors to assume the financial management role. As successor trustee you can do everything that the trust maker could do insofar as managing assets and taking care of his or her needs. You generally cannot change the terms of the trust, however. You, as successor trustee may be entitled to a fee for doing these things if it is authorized by the terms of the trust. These fees are taxable income to you, while monies you inherit at death are not.

So during the time of incapacity you sign the checks, prepare and file income taxes, manage repairs on property, run businesses, if any, and basically take care of all of the grantor's business and legal affairs. Unless you are also his guardian or medical power of attorney, you do not make decisions as to where he might live or whether a nursing home is appropriate, though you pay the bills for these things from his assets.

AT THE GRANTOR'S DEATH

Trust settlement is the term used to describe the process of wrapping up the affairs of the grantor after death and carrying out the instructions in the trust as to disposition of the trust assets. Attorneys are very good at trust settlement, and if you do not care about the cost of settling the trust or the amount of time it might take, the easiest way to settle a trust is to hire a lawyer.

The thing is that the work that needs to be done at death is not legal work. It is a mostly clerical job that almost anyone can do with some direction. Why pay lawyer rates at hundreds of dollars an hour for things you can easily do yourself? I am going to give you a step-by-step guide on how to settle a trust without a lawyer.

It's true that I do not recommend setting up your trust without a lawyer, but the trust settlement part is entirely different. A lawyer is usually not needed.

As discussed earlier, a trustee is a fiduciary, a person with a special responsibility both to the trust creditors and the trust heirs. If the trustee makes a mistake, he can be personally responsible for making good on it. That's why some trustees go ahead and hire the lawyer—to help cover their liability. If you as a trustee decide to hire a lawyer to help you, make sure she understands that you know the process and plan on doing as much of the work as possible yourself, leaving the lawyer with only lawyerly things to do. Do not let the lawyer talk you into letting her handle all the money and keep the checkbook. You or your accountant can pay the bills and write the checks.

THE SETTLEMENT PROCESS

Settling a trust consists of three steps:

1. Identify and collect the assets.
2. Identify and pay the debts and obligations.
3. Distribute the trust assets as directed in the trust document.

Seems pretty simple, and it is. Of course, there are many potential components to each step, but I am going to try to lay out the most common areas you are likely to encounter. If something comes up that is not covered here, you can always pay a trust attorney for a half-hour conference to ask a question or two. (You do not have to turn the trust over to him, though.) If you want a lot of detailed advice and basically to have the attorney settle the trust for you, then the attorney will need to read the trust carefully and likely will give you a written opinion letter. This is to ensure that he is giving you the right advice based upon the trust. He is legally liable if he gives you the wrong information or advice, so the services will likely be expensive.

Settlement of a trust after the death of one grantor in a joint trust is usually simple. The assets may stay in the trust under the continuing control and management of the survivor, who just has to take care of cashing in or rolling over beneficiary-type assets, and then nothing happens until the survivor dies. But this is not always the case, so I recommend being careful and looking for the following possible issues.

After the death of the first grantor to die, the survivor should do the following in relation to the trust.

Life Insurance. Contact the life insurance companies and request a claim form. This should then be filled out and returned to them with a certified copy of the death certificate. In most cases, the death benefit will be paid within thirty days.

Real Estate. If the real estate has previously been transferred to the joint trust by deed, nothing needs to be done since the trust is still in existence and still owns the real estate. As the surviving partner and surviving trustee, you are in charge of the trust and all trust assets, including the real estate. You may file a certified copy of the death certificate in the county where the property is located, but you are not required to do so at this time, and this may be done by your successor trustee at your death.

Personal Property. If the trust requires that certain personal property items of your partner's be transferred to named beneficiaries now rather than at your death, you, as the survivor, must now transfer those items to those persons. The balance of the personal property may be divided among the heirs in the proportionate shares, or if that is not workable, you may auction or sell the items and add the cash to the other accumulated assets.

Income Tax. The tax returns for the year of your spouse's death may be made as "married filing jointly" if you wish, but the last year's income tax return for your spouse must be filed.

Estate Tax. If the property and other assets of the trust, including property passing by beneficiary designation and property in the name of your spouse outside of the trust, exceed the estate tax exemption amount (currently $5,450,000, but subject to change), then you should consult your accountant or attorney about the need for filing a federal estate tax return Form 706. Even if no tax is due now, the filing of a return may still be required. It may also be necessary, if you had, for instance, an A/B trust, to obtain a separate Taxpayer Identification Number for the trust. In the case of an A/B trust, it is also very desirable to get provable valuations in place for all trust assets as of the date of death so that you can prove the values at that time. It can sometimes be difficult to establish a value at death for real estate or a business, for example, a year or two later.

State Inheritance Tax. Each state has a death tax separate from the federal tax. While only a few people will ever have to pay Federal Estate Tax based on the current rates, the state tax inheritance tax may have a much lower threshold. Ask your attorney about the law in your state, or do an Internet search for a general answer.

Benefits. Contact the Social Security office to see what survivor's benefits may be payable to the surviving spouse or children as well as to apply for the Social Security death benefit. Contact any previous employers to be certain that all employee benefits have been applied for. Form letters are included in the appendix to initiate this process.

Wrongful Death. If the death was or could have been the result of another person's negligence, such as medical malpractice or an auto accident, contact your attorney to see what benefits may be available for the family.

As was explained earlier, there are two basic types of trusts—the joint trust and the single trust. If you have a joint trust with a spouse, a parent, or a life partner, you should be sure that nothing has to be done at the death of one of you insofar as the trust is concerned. So in a joint trust, this is what might need to be done in some cases.

Read the Trust (Or Have Your Attorney Explain It to You)

The language of the trust document itself needs to be reviewed to see what happens to the trust at the death of one of the cograntors. Most often the trust will say that all the trust assets stay in trust and under the control of the surviving grantor. The survivor can still spend the money, borrow against the assets, sell them, or do anything that was possible before. The trust distribution provisions typically do not take effect until both grantors die. Often the surviving grantor has the ability to change the trust in any way desired. This is not always the case, so read the trust carefully.

There are numerous types of provisions that may take effect immediately upon the first death. Read the trust carefully to be sure you, as the surviving grantor, are doing everything correctly. It may be a good idea to go to the lawyer who prepared the trust to have her review the trust provisions with you. If you are making up your trust now, you may want to include some of these provisions in your trust, if they apply, or to remove the more onerous ones. Here are some examples:

1. Can you change the trust? Often in the case of blended families, the grantors want to be sure that if one of them dies first, the children of the first to die are not going to be disinherited by the survivor. So the trust may have a provision that the survivor may not change the trust in one or more ways. It becomes, in effect, wholly or partially irrevocable at the death of one. Even if the survivor can't change the beneficiaries, there may still be the power to make limited amendments, such as changing the successor trustees. If the trust is silent as to limitations on the right to amend after the death of one of you, the survivor can change the trust provisions in any way or even revoke the trust altogether.
2. A surviving grantor may discover from reading the document that while he cannot change the trust, he still retains the ability to remove assets from it or to make gifts. To thwart the no-amendment provision, the survivor might try to remove all the trust assets or give them away to effectively revoke the irrevocable trust. Provisions should be in the trust that prevent this sort of end-run around the rules.
3. There are sometimes family heirlooms or one-of-a-kind items that a grantor may want to see end up in the hands of his own heirs. Often a trust will instruct that these individual items go immediately to the people indicated without waiting for the death of the surviving grantor. Things like collections, jewelry, firearms, sporting goods, the family bible, collector cars, or other such possessions can be listed on an addendum to the trust that must be followed at the death of one person. However, the trust must specifically provide in its language that if such a list is appended to the document, it must be followed.
4. Trust property for the survivor. Often the family home is owned by one of the grantors prior to the beginning

of the relationship. The plan may be to pass the place on to the next generation after the death of the parent. The other partner may face undue hardship if forced to leave the house and find another place to live. Trusts often provide that the surviving grantor has the right to remain in the home for a set period of time (or for his lifetime), following which the property is given to the ultimate beneficiaries. In the meantime, either the trust pays the expenses on the property or, more commonly, the survivor is responsible for such things as taxes, insurance, maintenance, and utilities.

Again, if the trust is silent as to the residence, it remains part of the trust principal and belongs to the surviving partner, who can sell it, mortgage it, or even give it away.

And don't forget about the furniture and household goods. I had a case where the trust provided that the survivor had the right to live in the house but was silent as to the furniture. The children of the deceased grantor, who were the ultimate beneficiaries, removed all of it. So while the survivor had the right to live in the house, he had to buy all new furniture, silverware, pots and pans, and even bath towels. A trust provision could cover that kind of situation.

5. New trustees. To make sure the trust provisions are followed, careful grantors will sometimes provide that at the death of one of them, the surviving grantor is no longer solely in charge of the trust management. Often a bank or one of the deceased grantor's children will be added as a cotrustee along with the surviving grantor.

This is not necessarily a bad thing, since it ensures that the survivor has no choice but to honor the terms of the trust, but it could make for complications on the part of the survivor. From that point on, the survivor has to agree on all financial decisions with the new cotrustee. I had a client whose husband died, and the trust appointed his daughter as the cotrustee with the wife. While the husband was alive, the client thought the plan would work fine, but after he died, the stepdaughter made every effort to conserve all the trust assets, refusing or complicating every request for money from the trust.

Her thinking was that the stepmother was spending the ultimate inheritance. The courts could have intervened to appoint a new trustee, but this would have added another layer of cost and complexity to the process. Adding a trustee to serve along with your partner is a good idea in theory, but in practice it can lead to rather contentious situations. Be careful what provisions are put in the trust, since they are very difficult (if not impossible) to change, and your cograntor will have to live with them.

6. Changing trust asset management. At the death of one grantor, some trusts will have provisions that put the survivor on what amounts to an allowance. A new trustee is in charge of paying the bills for the surviving partner. The survivor gets her expenses paid for life, but at death, the trust assets pass on to the heirs named in the trust. There is no right to the use of the principal, except in limited amounts and circumstances. These provisions are typically put in for estate tax purposes but sometimes to preserve the assets in the trust for the ultimate beneficiaries. When you set up your trust, be sure that you understand the effect these provisions will have on the survivor. Most often the surviving partner resents having limitations on access to what was once jointly owned property.
7. Tax provisions. Years ago, when estate taxes were assessed on estates of $600,000 and up, estate tax provisions were a valuable part of any good trust. Now, the threshold is

$5.45 million, so this is not an issue for nearly everyone. The problem is that many trusts were created a long time ago and have not been brought up to date to reflect the new laws. Consequently, some surviving grantors find themselves subject to restrictions on their access to the joint trust assets that serve no tax-saving purpose yet severely limit their financial activities.

The "QTIP" provision is a common one. This acronym stands for "qualified terminable interest property." It's a mouthful, and a detailed explanation is beyond the scope and intent of this book. Briefly, this trust provision has been used to avoid estate taxes and is still used for the larger estates that may exceed the $5.45 million threshold.

Here's how it works. Each grantor has today what amounts to a $5.45 million exemption from estate tax. The problem in larger estates is that if one grantor dies before the other, the survivor gets all of the assets tax-free (due to the unlimited marital deduction); but then at the death of the survivor, there would be only one estate tax deduction left. So at today's tax rates, a $6.45 million estate could end up paying four hundred thousand dollars in federal estate taxes. The QTIP provision in a trust could solve that problem by allowing the taxable portion over the exemption amount to be placed in a separate account. The survivor could draw the interest, and in some cases, part of the principal each year from that account, and then at the death of the survivor, the remainder would go to the ultimate beneficiaries. That way the survivor would have one exemption, and the first to die would have his exemption preserved to shield the QTIP amount from estate taxes. In effect, this doubles the estate tax exemption to $10.9 million, so at death there would be no estate taxes whatsoever.

Sounds good, but some poorly drafted trusts will require that a certain portion of the trust assets be put into a QTIP share, even if there is no tax problem due to the size of the total trust estate. A $2.5 million estate would have no federal tax liability, yet some trusts will put half of it into the restrictive QTIP anyway. (While it was common years ago for most states to have a separate state inheritance tax, most states now use a so-called pickup tax, which allows them a share of the federal tax collected. A half dozen states still retain some form of inheritance tax with varying exemption levels. Contact your accountant or use the Internet to look up the rules in your state.)

Another big problem area is the older A/B trusts, sometimes called marital and family trusts. These act very much like the QTIP in that they divide the trust into separate shares, and the spouse gets the marital share without restriction and has limited access to the family share. The older ones sometimes have language requiring that all the trust assets that do not qualify for the marital deduction go to the family trust to preserve an estate tax exemption on taxable estates. However, the marital deduction is now unlimited, which means that under the terms of the trust, all the assets would go to the marital trust and there would be no tax savings by preserving the deduction of the first to die.

There are a lot of kinds of trusts, often with very complex provisions that even lawyers have a hard time deciphering. Be sure you completely understand all the provisions that are going to govern your access to your own money before you let a lawyer put them in the document. As discussed earlier, some lawyers may be using form software that already contains the provisions, and they may be in your document whether they are appropriate for your situation or not.

The lesson here is that if you find these complicated tax provisions in the trust you are about to administer, or if you are the surviving grantor, it is wise to see a trust attorney (not just any old attorney) to find out how this affects you and what you need to do. It may be that you will have to immediately begin partial administration of the trust even before the death of the cograntor because of the need to carry out instructions in the trust that take effect at the death of the first to die.

If both grantors are liable for a debt, such as a mortgage, then the survivor can continue to make any required payments just as before. Most contracts do not have an acceleration clause at the death of one debtor. However, if a grantor dies and the cograntor is not jointly liable for the debt, it must be paid off in full out of the trust assets. As an example, I have seen cases where only one person who had signed on a mortgage dies. The survivor has no legal right to continue to make the mortgage payments but must either pay it off or refinance. This is what you might call a due-on-death clause.

So credit cards, auto loans, taxes, and even mortgages in only the name of the deceased are due and payable in full out of trust assets, provided they are not joint debts. If you discover that your partner had debts in her own name, then they must be paid at death from the trust assets, even if those assets were mostly put in the trust by the survivor. This was referenced earlier in this book, and the remedy sometimes is to have separate trusts for each partner.

ADDITIONAL STEPS TO TAKE WHEN SOMEONE DIES

After the funeral and burial details have been carried out, there are other things that need to be done when a partner dies. The following apply to the death of one grantor of a joint trust, the surviving grantor's death, and the death of a sole grantor of a single-person trust.

1. Order at least a dozen death certificates. It is easier to get several at first than it is to get more later, and they will be needed for various purposes. When you give these out, see if a photocopy will suffice, since a certified death certificate can cost $25 or more. You may need them for life insurance claims, Social Security benefits, VA benefits, probate of the will if necessary, and pension or profit-sharing plans, as well as a copy to include with federal or state estate tax returns.
2. Cancel credit cards that were just in the name of the deceased or in the name of his or her business. As a practical matter, even though these should be paid off in full at death, if the card is no longer being used and there is not enough ready cash to pay them, you may be able to get an agreement to continue the payments. You should never use the cards yourself unless you are an authorized signer.
3. Similarly, cancel other services such as debit cards, telephone and cell-phone accounts, Internet services and subscriptions, automatic payments from credit cards and bank accounts, cable television, and other recurring expenses that are only in the name of the deceased. They may require a copy of a death certificate to process the cancellation.
4. Keep up payments to maintain real estate (such as utilities, taxes, and insurance) until the property can be sold or transferred. We have had incredibly expensive repairs required when the gas and electric were cut off on vacant property and the water pipes froze and broke. The trustee is responsible for managing and preserving the property of the trust and could be held liable for failing to do so.

   This would be only for property separately in the name of the deceased. Jointly owned property or property in the joint trust will continue to be under the control and management of the survivor, so the survivor would continue to maintain the trust properties.

FINDING ASSETS

1. Contact employers for information on benefit programs. There may be unpaid vacation pay, the last paycheck, life insurance, retirement accounts, or profit-sharing benefits that would accrue to either the trust or the person's family or estate.
2. File claims for life insurance and other death benefit accounts such as annuities. This is a very simple process of filling in a claim form and returning it to the insurance company with a death certificate. The insurance proceeds would be payable to the named beneficiary, which we would hope to be the trust. It may be necessary to open a bank account in the name of the trust in which to deposit the check if you have not already opened one for the joint trust. See these instructions to get a trust tax identification number, which you will need to open the account. Remember, too, that some credit card companies offer free life insurance to their cardholders. If there are loans due, find out whether the deceased had credit life insurance to cover these. The original loan paperwork will usually tell you this.
3. File claims for retirement accounts. Things like IRAs, 401(k)s, 403(b)s, tax-deferred annuities, and myriad other assets have beneficiaries. The claim would be filed on behalf of the beneficiary, and the plan administrator will provide information on what elections are available to the beneficiaries. A spouse as a beneficiary, for example, may be able to roll over the account into an IRA in his or her own name, thereby continuing to defer the tax owed. Filing the claim is just a matter of filling out a form according to its written instructions. The company representative will typically help you with this.

4. If the deceased is a veteran, contact the VA office for what benefits may be available. A form letter is included in the appendix for that purpose.
5. Contact any organizations to which the deceased belonged and see if there are any benefits available. Some of them may have insurance programs for their members. Again, there is a form letter for you to use in the appendix.
6. Try to identify any online accounts the deceased may have had. Sometimes there are substantial assets in accounts through E-Trade, Scottrade, and other online brokerage or banking accounts. There are even online gambling accounts some people have in which they keep deposits. Similarly, there may be accounts for commodities, such as money invested in gold funds.
7. Look for refundable deposits with utility companies or landlords.
8. If auto insurance or homeowner insurance is canceled, there may be refunds of unearned premium due to you as the trustee of the estate. It is a good idea to talk to the insurance agent of the deceased, who can help with identifying other assets.
9. Contact banks and credit unions to be sure all accounts are in the name of the joint trust, and, if not, see if they have a "pay on death" designation or a beneficiary naming you or the trust as the owner at death. The bank will want a death certificate. If there are accounts that exist just in the name of the deceased with no beneficiary on them, they must be transferred via the pour-over will to the trust using, ideally, the small estate probate procedure in your state.
10. Identify business interests. If the deceased had business interests such as partnerships, sole proprietorships, LLCs, or corporations, these would typically already be in the name of the trust. If there are others involved,

there may be partnership agreements or buy-out agreements, which would pay the estate of the deceased for the share of the business value. Businesses may be continued or sold depending upon the feasibility of either approach and the instructions of the deceased.

11. Search the house. Look through desk drawers and paperwork for evidence of insurance policies, savings bonds, or other assets. I once found a manila envelope on a bookshelf crammed with other paperwork in the house of a person whose estate I was settling. Inside was a paid-up insurance policy with a cash value of more than a quarter million dollars. It was a fluke that I ran across this, but it ended up being a big surprise to the family. It is not unusual for people to hide valuables in their home, though they can be difficult to find sometimes. If there is a family safe, be sure that the successor trustee knows the combination. It is a shame to have to destroy a perfectly good safe to get it open because no one knows how to get into it. Contrary to what you see at the movies, it is not always possible to have some gizmo figure out the combination. The last time I had a safe company assist in opening a safe, they ended up doing it with two big men, a sledgehammer, and a large pry bar.
12. Though not as commonly used today, some people still have safe deposit boxes at their banks. If the box is in the name of the trust, or if there is another authorized signer, you may be able to access the box without involving the courts simply by presenting the death certificate.
13. The decedent's mail should be forwarded to the trustee. Watch the mail carefully, since you may discover statements sent out quarterly or annually, revealing assets of which you were unaware. Bills will be coming in, too, usually by mail.
14. Internet accounts may not have mailed statements, ever. So look on computer credit card accounts for

debit transactions that may identify accounts or other assets.

15. The grantor might have owned websites or domain names. These could have considerable value as well. Try to find the grantor's list of user names and passwords, and go over his search history on his computer to further investigate unknown assets.

VALUING ASSETS

Most assets are easily valued since they will be converted to cash immediately after the death of the deceased. Some assets, though, will be kept intact in a joint trust situation, and a verifiable appraisal may be a valuable tool later on. Real estate, for example, may be part of a potentially taxable estate. The value at date of death may have to be proven to show either the amount of estate tax owed or that a tax return was not needed because the value kept the estate below the threshold for taxation. Valuation, which is provable, is also used to establish a value as of date of death for capital gains tax purposes to establish a new tax basis for the assets.

When assets are to be divided on a percentage basis among several heirs and some things are to be given out individually without liquidating them, we need to be able to prove the value in order to show how much of the person's share who received the asset was represented by it. For example, it is common to have collections, antiques, or other personal property items left to a particular heir with the understanding that the item is to be considered part of her share of the estate. We do not want an argument over the value of the share, and an appraisal solves the problem.

INCOME TAXES

An income tax return must be filed for the deceased for the year of death if there was taxable income. Even if there wasn't any income tax liability, the deceased may have been eligible for certain local, state, or federal tax rebates or credits that could be claimed by filing the return. Also, pay attention to any estimated tax payments that may have been made by the deceased. Always find the deceased's last year income tax return and contact the preparer to see what issues may exist or for help in filing the last return.

If you are the surviving spouse, you may file a joint return for the year of death. Talk to your accountant about the best plan for you.

NOTIFYING EVERYONE

Part of the obligation of the trustee is to notify creditors and heirs of the death and of the existence of the trust.

In a joint trust, the heirs do not need to be notified unless they are to receive something immediately or if the trust document calls for it. The trustee would notify them after both trust grantors are gone.

Notification of heirs is typically done by sending a letter and a copy of the trust to each heir. In some states, there is only the obligation to send the portion of the trust that pertains to that particular heir. From then on, the heirs must be kept updated on what assets are in the estate and what expenses come out of the estate. This can be done at the time the assets are distributed, unless it drags on for some reason, in which case annual reports should be provided. Good communication lessens complaints to the trustee by heirs.

Notification of creditors is a bit different. In a trust, we want to be able to settle matters quickly, without the fear of an unknown creditor presenting a claim after the assets have been distributed to the heirs. In some states this is an easy matter. Michigan, for instance, allows a trustee to publish a notice in the newspaper called a "Notice to Creditors," which lets everyone know that there has been a death and allows any unknown creditors a limited amount of time (in this case, four months) to present their claim before they are forever barred from bringing it up later. This gives the trust a short statute of limitations and allows the trust to be closed up quickly and safely.

Known creditors must be contacted individually either by paying the debts or by sending notice of the death so that they can bill the trust for what is due. It is a good practice to send all doctors, clinics, and hospitals, as well as other health-care providers, a copy of the Notice to Known Creditors to put them on notice to get their billings to you or they will not be paid. Hospitals are notorious for sending medical bills months after services are provided.

PAYING THE DEBTS AND EXPENSES

Now the assets are known and the debts are all totaled. If sufficient funds are available, go ahead and pay the debts in full, keeping statements and receipts for your records. If the debts exceed the assets, we have a problem.

State laws set up rules on how claims are to be paid in probate cases if there are insufficient funds, and, in some states, the same rules apply to trusts. These laws refer to "priority of claims." Here is a common set of rules:

> If the applicable estate property is insufficient to pay all claims and allowances in full, the personal representative shall make payment in the following order of priority:
>
> a. Costs and expenses of administration.
> b. Reasonable funeral and burial expenses.
> c. Homestead allowance.
> d. Family allowance.
> e. Exempt property.
> f. Debts and taxes with priority under federal law, including, but not limited to, medical assistance payments that are subject to adjustment or recovery from an estate under section 1917 of the Social Security Act, 42 USC 1396p.

g. Reasonable and necessary medical and hospital expenses of the decedent's last illness, including a compensation of persons attending the decedent.
h. Debts and taxes with priority under other laws of this state.
i. All other claims.

The "all other claims" would then be paid pro rata at so many cents on the dollar after dividing the total remaining assets by the remaining debts to get the ratio.

A point that might help you in a situation with more debts than assets is that the first priority is costs and expenses of administration, which includes the fees of the trustee and/or personal representative. If you are the surviving partner, you can charge a fee, usually hourly, for everything you do to settle the estate, the money for which comes off the top. Check state law, of course, to be sure this works where you live, and check the language of the trust, which may spell out what the trustee fees would be. In most cases, the debts will not exceed the assets, so everything can be paid in full.

TAX IDENTIFICATION NUMBERS

A Tax Identification Number for a living person is his Social Security Number. That number cannot be used after death, so a Tax Identification Number should be obtained for the trust itself. With that number, the trustee may open bank accounts, cash checks payable to the trust, and put in claims for trust assets. It once was a lengthy process to get a Tax ID Number using the IRS Form SS-4. Not anymore. These can be obtained online by going to the IRS website and filling out the online form. The number will be provided immediately. Alternatively, you can call a toll-free number or fill out the SS-4 and apply by fax. The IRS calls these Employer Identification Numbers, even though for a trust there is no employer. Here is the contact information, current as of the time this book went to press.

Website:
www.irs.gov/businesses/small/article/0,,id=97860,00.html

Text from website:

APPLY ONLINE

The Internet EIN application is the preferred method for customers to apply for and obtain an EIN. Once the application is completed, the information is validated during the online session, and an EIN is issued immediately. The online application process is available for all entities whose principal business, office, or agency, or legal residence (in the case of an individual), is located in the United States or US Territories. The principal officer, general partner, grantor, owner, trustor, etc. must have a valid Taxpayer Identification Number (Social Security Number, Employer Identification Number, or Individual Taxpayer Identification Number) in order to use the online application.

APPLY BY EIN TOLL-FREE TELEPHONE SERVICE

Taxpayers can obtain an EIN immediately by calling the Business & Specialty Tax Line at (800) 829-4933. The hours of operation are 7:00 a.m.–10:00 p.m. local time, Monday through Friday. An assistor takes the information, assigns the EIN, and provides the number to an authorized individual over the telephone. Note: International applicants must call (215) 516-6999 (not a toll-free number).

APPLY BY FAX

Taxpayers can fax the completed Form SS-4 (PDF) application to their state fax number (see Where to File—Business Forms and Filing Addresses), after ensuring that the Form SS-4 contains all of the required information. If it is determined that the entity needs a new EIN, one will be assigned using the appropriate procedures for the entity type. If the taxpayer's fax number is provided, a fax will be sent back with the EIN within four (4) business days.

APPLY BY MAIL

The processing timeframe for an EIN application received by mail is four weeks. Ensure that the Form SS-4 (PDF) contains all of the required information. If it is determined that the entity needs a new EIN, one will be assigned using the appropriate procedures for the entity type and mailed to the taxpayer.

OTHER IMPORTANT INFORMATION

Thirty-Party Authorization

The Third Party Designee section must be completed at the bottom of the Form SS-4. The Form SS-4 must also be signed by the taxpayer for the third-party designee authorization to be valid. The Form SS-4 must be mailed or faxed to the appropriate service center. A third-party designee may call for an EIN; however, a faxed Form SS-4, with the taxpayer's signature, is still required. IRS assistors will take the information over the phone from the third-party designee and ask the third party to fax the completed Form SS-4 to them (to the IRS assistor's attention) at an administrative fax number. After receiving the faxed Form SS-4, the EIN will be assigned and faxed back to the third-party designee or given over the phone. The third-party designee's authority terminates at the time the EIN is assigned and released to the designee.

The EIN is also used to file tax returns for the trust itself. IRS Form 1041 is a trust tax return that must be filed for every year that the trust has income. Often money is held in investments for a period of time before it is passed out to the beneficiaries. This may be because the trust provides for scheduled distributions to beneficiaries rather than a lump sum, or it may be a trust that is being managed for the lifetime of a beneficiary or group of beneficiaries. The trust must report the income to the IRS, and an EIN is necessary to do that.

DISTRIBUTING THE ASSETS

After all the assets are gathered together and the debts are paid, it is time to distribute the assets left in the trust according to the trust instructions. For most trusts this is merely a matter of writing checks to the heirs in the shares dictated by the trust document. Sometimes, though, all the assets have not been liquidated and money is just sitting in an account waiting, for instance, for the sale of that last piece of real estate. As the trustee, you do not have to wait for every single asset to be converted to cash before you start divvying up the shares.

Partial distributions can be made. The trustee may, for example, hand out 90 percent of the trust assets, hold back 10 percent to cover the final tax return or to pay expenses on that house that hasn't sold yet, and then make a final distribution when everything is complete. The amount of a partial distribution would depend on the expected future expenses. You don't want to hand the money out and then try to get everyone to chip in when an unexpected trust expense occurs.

Get receipts. In the appendix is a Receipt for Distributive Share form. This should be signed by each heir when he or she receives a distribution and kept by the trustee. The form provides protections for the trustee so that there are no complaints later on.

THE TRUST THAT CONTINUES AFTER DEATH

Trusts do not always end as soon as the assets are identified and the debts are paid. Often the trust acts as an asset manager for some or all heirs. Children, disabled heirs, and spendthrifts may find the trustee controlling their trust funds for them for a period of years, until they reach a certain age, or even for their lifetime. How does the trustee set up this sort of trust and manage the funds?

After identifying the assets, paying the bills, giving out the personal things to those who are to get them, and distributing shares to those whose trust share is not going to continue to be held in trust, the next step is to begin following the instructions of the trust grantor to manage assets for the remaining beneficiaries.

1. Get a Tax ID Number for the trust if you have not already done so. How to get one is explained earlier in this chapter.
2. Invest the assets that are to be managed for the trust beneficiary. As a trustee you are required to make safe, conservative investments. The rule generally is the "prudent investor rule," which means you must diversify the investments and not do anything risky that could jeopardize them. My recommendation is to contact an investment advisor, such as one of the large brokerage houses or a certified financial planner, and have that advisor set up a diversified portfolio for the trust, allowing you the ability to access the assets as needed to pay the expenses of the trust beneficiary. Recurring payments such as utilities or medical insurance can be set up on an automatic pay system so the trustee is not burdened with writing monthly checks. If the financial planner is handling the payouts it may take no more effort than a telephone call to direct an extraordinary payment for the benefit of the trust beneficiary. The job of trustee, once the accounts are set up, should not be difficult.

For example, if you are the trustee for a trust for minor children with the provisions that the money may be used for their support, maintenance, education, and medical needs, you will need to be able to direct payments from the trust assets for these purposes. If there is more than one child benefiting from the trust, you would direct the broker to set up separate asset accounts for each child so that each is drawing from his own share of the total. (Some trusts may let everyone draw from the same pot of assets, so there would be only one asset account.) Typically, the balance of a child's share not used for the permitted purposes would be turned over to that child upon her reaching the age specified in the trust, such as twenty-five. A trust for a disabled person might have to continue for the person's lifetime but would be invested and managed the same way.

Any trust that continues beyond the death of the grantor becomes a separate legal taxpaying entity. The trustee must file an income tax return for the trust every year just as if the trust were a real person or a company.

The trust must come to an end at some point. Most states have a law called the "rule against perpetuities." This law means that a trust may not be perpetual and that at some point all the trust assets have to be given to someone. This rule is flexible, since the typical one allows a trust to stay in place for "a life in being plus twenty-one years." So if you had two children and two grandchildren and wanted to set up a trust that provided the income to your children for life, then their children for their lifetimes, then to your great grandchildren for twenty-one years, the trust could stay in existence for that long without violating the rule.

The rule against perpetuities does not in all states apply to all assets that may be placed in trust, nor is it a rule everywhere. It may only apply to real estate, for example, when a person wants to keep the cottage in the family. Check with your lawyer if you want to set up this type of trust provision or if you are the trustee of a trust with the provision in it.

APPENDIX A

Forms and Form Letters

The following form letters and forms are provided for educational purposes and are not intended to act as legal advice. While these work for most areas, I cannot guarantee what particular rules and laws may be required where you live. Often organizations will respond to a form letter by sending you their own forms to fill out, so these may act to help initiate the process rather than completing it. Before relying on these, be sure to get the advice of an attorney in your area.

The addresses were current at press time, but should be checked. These letters may be too small to photocopy, but retyping is easy enough.

1. Notice to Creditors: Decedent's Trust Estate. (This is published once in the local newspaper where the deceased lived. In some states, publishing this notice creates a short statute of limitations for potential or unknown creditors. Ask your attorney about the legal efficacy of this form in the jurisdiction of the deceased.)

2. Funeral and Burial Arrangements. (You, as the grantor, should fill out this form for the use of your trustee so that your wishes are known and any prepaid items are revealed to the family.)
3. Obituary. (This is a matter of personal preference and local custom. Often funeral homes will have formats, but this gives you a place to start.)
4. Letter to Life Insurance Company.
5. Letter to Social Security.
6. Letter to Health Insurance Company.
7. Letter to Veteran's Administration.
8. Letter to Organization. (Often membership organizations have group benefit programs that may offer death benefits or services to the family.)
9. Letter to Civil Service Commission.
10. Letter to Employer.
11. Receipt for Distributive Share. (To be signed by any beneficiary and retained by the trustee as a receipt when the trustee distributes assets.)

NOTICE TO CREDITORS
DECEDENT'S TRUST ESTATE

TRUST ESTATE OF _____
(name of deceased)

To all creditors:

NOTICE TO CREDITORS: The decedent, _____
(name of deceased)

who lived at

_____,
(address of deceased)

died on _____ 20 ____ .

Creditors of the decedent are notified that all claims against the trust estate will be forever barred unless presented to _____, the successor trustee named in The _____ Revocable
(name of deceased)
Living Trust established by decedent on the _____ day of _____, 20____.
All such claims must be presented to the said successor trustee within 4 months after the date of publication of this notice.

_____ _____
Date Trustee Name

_____
Address

_____
Telephone

PUBLISH ABOVE INFORMATION ONLY

Publish one time in _____

Name of Newspaper

Furnish Affidavit of Publication and statement of publication charges to the trustee whose address is above.

FUNERAL AND BURIAL ARRANGEMENTS

Prepaid items and location, also include location of supporting paperwork:

Item Location _____

Cemetery Lot _____

Headstone _____

Funeral Services/Supplies _____

Persons or Organizations to notify (including Veterans Administration and organizations such as Masons who you may want to be involved in the funeral ceremony. You may want to attach a list of other people with contact information if these are not known by your family.)

_____

_____

_____

_____

Church or religious organization to which you belong

_____

Who would you like to officiate at a funeral ceremony?

_____

Specific burial instructions (such as whether or not you want cremation or where you would like to be buried)

_____

Cemetery plot location (or desired location to purchase a plot)

_____

Deed to plot location if any is located

_____

Church/synagogue to notify

_____

Date _____ Your Signature _____

OBITUARY

An obituary has several standard formats, varying by region of the country, religious orientation, and family tradition. Most newspapers will print whatever you decide to write. Some papers run these for free, while others charge you based on how long the obituary is and how many days it is to run.

Here is the traditional simplified format, though this can run longer or even shorter.

> John William Jones, age 89, died Saturday, March 12, in Ann Arbor, Michigan.
> Services will be held at the Moore Funeral Home on March 16 at 2:00 PM followed by burial at Sunset Gardens Park where a graveside service will be held.
> John was a member of Westside Church and retired from Ford Motor Company. He is survived by his wife Barbara and his two children Nathan and Kristine.
>
> Memorial contributions may be made to the National Heart Fund.

LETTER TO LIFE INSURANCE COMPANY

Date _____

Name and Address of Insurance Company

Dear Sir or Madam:

Re: _____
Insert Name of Deceased

Date of Death _____

The above-named person had a policy with your company.

Policy Number _____

Please send me information on the death benefits or accrued benefits during the lifetime of the deceased and all claim forms needed to claim these benefits.

Please let me know what other information or documents you may need me to provide.

_____
Your Signature

_____
Print Name
Your Address
Your Telephone and Email

LETTER TO SOCIAL SECURITY

Date _____

Social Security Administration
Address of Local Social Security Office

Dear Sir or Madam:

Re: _____
Insert Name of Deceased

Date of Death _____

Social Security Number _____

I am writing to inform you of the death of the above person. A copy of the death certificate is enclosed. I would like to arrange a meeting to discuss the options and benefits available to the surviving spouse and/or family.

Please either call me or let me know how to proceed to set up such a meeting.

Thank you for your help.

_____
Your Signature

_____
Print Name
Your Address
Your Telephone and Email

LETTER TO HEALTH INSURANCE COMPANY

Date _____

Name and Address of Insurance Company

Dear Sir or Madam:

Re: _____
Insert Name of Deceased

Date of Death _____

The above-named person had a policy with your company.

Policy Number _____

Please send me information on the death benefits or accrued benefits during the lifetime of the deceased and all claim forms needed to claim these benefits.

Please let me know what other information or documents you may need me to provide.

_____
Your Signature

_____
Print Name
Your Address
Your Telephone and Email

LETTER TO VETERAN'S ADMINISTRATION

Date _____

Veteran's Administration
Insurance Division
500 Wissachickon Avenue or Fort Snelling
Philadelphia, PA 19010 St. Paul, MN 55111

Re: _____
Insert Name of Deceased

Date of Death _____

Dear Sir or Madam:

I represent the estate of the above-named person whose Social Security Number is _____ .

I have enclosed a photocopy of the death certificate.

He may have had insurance or other benefits due to him; please let me know what was available and the forms or procedures to claim those benefits.

The information I have is as follows:

Branch of Service _____

Date of Entering Service _____

Discharge Date _____

Service Number (if different than Social Security Number)

_____

Please let me know what other information or documents you may need me to provide.

_____

Your Signature

_____

Print Name
Your Address
Your Telephone and Email

LETTER TO ORGANIZATION

Date _____

Name and Address of Organization

Re: _____
Insert Name of Deceased

Date of Death _____

Dear Sir or Madam:

I represent the estate of the above-named person whose Social Security Number is _____ .

I have enclosed a photocopy of the death certificate.

Please let me know what benefits may be available to the deceased and/or his family, including such things as life insurance, disability, vacation and sick pay, retirement, or other benefits. If there are claim forms for these please send them to me or let me know how to get them.

Please let me know what other information or documents you may need.

Sincerely,

_____
Your Signature

_____
Print Name
Your Address
Your Telephone and Email

LETTER TO CIVIL SERVICE COMMISSION

(Date) _____

Civil Service Commission
1900 East Street, N.W.
Washington, D.C. 20415

Re: _____
Insert Name of Deceased

Date of Death _____

Dear Sir or Madam:

I represent the estate of the above-named person whose Social Security Number is _____.

I have enclosed a photocopy of the death certificate.

Please let me know what benefits may be available to the deceased and/or his family, including such things as life insurance, disability, vacation and sick pay, retirement, or other benefits. If there are claim forms for these please send them to me or let me know how to get them.

Please let me know what other information or documents you may need.

Sincerely,

_____
Your Signature

_____
Print Name
Your Address
Your Telephone and Email

LETTER TO EMPLOYER

(Date) _____

Name of Employer _____
Address _____
_____

Dear Sir or Madam:

I represent the estate of your employee/former employee whose name is _____ and whose Social Security Number is _____.

Please let me know if there are any accrued and unpaid benefits available to him or payable to his estate. This might include unpaid vacation or sick pay, group life insurance, pension or retirement benefits, stock options or stock purchase plans, profit sharing, disability income, payroll savings, or any other benefits. If the deceased left personal property in your possession, please let me know how to arrange for pickup.

Also, if there are claim forms available to access these benefits, could you please forward those or tell me how to get them.

I have enclosed a photocopy of the death certificate.

Please let me know what other information or documents you may need.

Sincerely,

_____
Your Signature

_____
Print Name
Your Address
Your Telephone and Email

RECEIPT FOR DISTRIBUTIVE SHARE

I hereby acknowledge the receipt of the following asset(s) from the following trust estate:

_____:

Name and Date of Trust

Description of asset(s) received:

This is a _____ full or _____ partial distribution to me from the estate.

I acknowledge that I have received a copy of the trust document as well as an accounting of trust assets and expenditures to date and am satisfied with the same.

Dated: _____

_____

Signature

_____

Print Name

APPENDIX B

Short Form: Guide to Trust Funding

See the information in this section for detailed instructions and letters of instruction for various types of assets. This list covers most things for most people.

Below are some guidelines on transferring some kinds of property to a trust. If you have property not listed below, contact the institution in charge of it and ask about their procedure or look in the detailed instructions. Keep in mind that each company you deal with will have its own procedure, forms, and preferred language they use when making transfers to your trust, so be prepared to be flexible. They will want to see your certificate of trust existence or the trust itself. It is okay to give them a copy, but under no circumstances let them keep the original.

In general, transfers of assets to the trust will be done as follows:

1. Transfer directly into the name of the trust. The assets (such as real estate, bank accounts, CDs, money mar-

kets, and stocks) will be in the name of your trust rather than in your name. You will contact the institution and request this change (using, for example, the General Account Transfer Letter in your packet), and the institution will change the ownership of the account or asset to the name of the trust.

2. Life insurance is changed by changing the primary beneficiary to the name of the trust if you want it to be part of the trust assets.
3. Tax-deferred assets, such as IRAs, 401(k)s, TIAACREF, 403(b)s, etc., depend upon several things. If you are married, the spouse normally remains the primary beneficiary in order to retain all rollover elections in an easy manner. The trust would be the second or alternate beneficiary if you want these assets controlled by the trust; otherwise you can directly name the second beneficiary and leave these out of the trust. Typically if you have children, you will want the trust as the second beneficiary rather than the children. A single person will either name the trust as primary beneficiary or an individual person. You can discuss this with your attorney or financial advisor. Payout elections may still be available to beneficiaries if the trust provisions are complete using the "look through" provisions of the IRS code.
4. Certain credit union and bank accounts, brokerage accounts—particularly those with direct deposit—and pension and Social Security accounts may be more easily handled by a "pay on death" (POD) or "transfer on death" (TOD) designation. A transfer form is included herein for that purpose. (Credit unions sometimes require this procedure because some do not allow trusts to own accounts.)
5. Automobiles, motorcycles, boats, trailers, and other things with titles can be put into the trust name at the Secretary of State's office or tax office—whatever it is

called in your jurisdiction—if there are no liens on the titles. Sometimes there is an alternate way to transfer titles. If there is to be no probate—and there would not be with a fully funded trust—the state may transfer titles to the next of kin merely by seeing the death certificate and signing their affidavit.

Personal property such as furniture and household goods, jewelry, collections, animals, tools, farm equipment, or other tangible assets without titles will be part of the trust by virtue of the Assignment of Assets form, which is part of every well-written trust.

APPENDIX C

Decision-Making for Your Estate Plan Form

Filling out this form will be very helpful to you in preparing your legal documents. The types of decisions that need to be made are listed with, in some cases, suggestions. By picking from the options before you see an attorney you will have time to discuss and think about the appropriate choices. This will save you attorney time, and money, later on. Your attorney likely would ask you these things, but having answers prepared ahead of time will make the process quicker.

YOUR NAME _____

US Citizen? ____ Yes ____ No

Date of Birth _____ Email _____

SPOUSE'S NAME _____

US Citizen? ____ Yes ____ No

Date of Birth _____ Email _____

Telephone You _____ Spouse _____

Street Address _____
City_____County_____
State _____ Zip _____

Mailing Address if different

_____

_____

Children of this marriage if any: (Including those deceased)
Name: _____
DOB ___/___/___ Living? Yes ___ No ___
Name: _____
DOB ___/___/___ Living? Yes ___ No ___
Name: _____
DOB ___/___/___ Living? Yes ___ No ___
Name: _____
DOB ___/___/___ Living? Yes ___ No ___
Name: _____
DOB ___/___/___ Living? Yes ___ No ___
Name: _____
DOB ___/___/___ Living? Yes ___ No ___

Children of a prior marriage: (Including those deceased) check if children of H=husband W=wife
Name: _____ H ___ W
DOB ___/___/___ Living? Yes ___ No ___
Name: _____ H ___ W
DOB ___/___/___ Living? Yes ___ No ___
Name: _____ H ___ W
DOB ___/___/___ Living? Yes ___ No ___
Name: _____ H ___ W
DOB ___/___/___ Living? Yes ___ No ___
Name: _____ H ___ W
DOB ___/___/___ Living? Yes ___ No ___

Name: _____ H ___ W
DOB ___/___/___ Living? Yes ___ No ___

Are any children disabled, under a court-ordered guardianship, or receiving governmental assistance such as Medicaid? If so, explain:

_____

_____

Is your spouse disabled, in a nursing home, or suffering from dementia, Alzheimer's disease, or other mental impairment? If so, explain:

_____

_____

If so, do you have a durable power of attorney for your spouse? _____ If so, please attach a copy.

If you have minor children, who would you like to nominate as their guardians (do not name a couple):
First Choice: _____
Relationship to you _____
Second Choice: _____
Relationship to you _____

(The reason we do not suggest a couple as guardians is that it is possible they could be separated or contemplating divorce at your death, and if both are named, then there is a potential custody case that could result.)

Trustees. Who do you want to handle your estate after both of your deaths? (Name one or more.)
In Order _____ Jointly _____
1)
Name: _____

Address _____

_____

Relationship to you _____

Telephone _____

2)

Name: _____

Address _____

_____

Relationship to you _____

Telephone _____

3)

Name: _____

Address _____

_____

Relationship to you _____

Telephone _____

Your beneficiaries. This is the section of your trust that is of most interest to everyone and which deserves the most thought. Sometimes the decision is simple, leaving everything to one person or leaving everything equally to a group of people. But there are situations where that distribution plan would not be in the best interests of the beneficiaries. Here are some ideas:

If your beneficiaries include minor children, it is a very good idea to restrict their access to their inheritance subject to certain conditions. Here is an example of one such plan.

If any Beneficiary (including but not limited to a grandchild, if any) is under the age of 40 years when the distribution is to be made, the Trustee shall retain any such property and administer and distribute the same for the benefit of the beneficiary, paying to or for the benefit of such person so much of the income and principal of the retained property from time to time, as the Trustee deems advisable for his or her health, education, support, and maintenance.

Note that this language allows the trustee to use his discretion on what he thinks is appropriate for the beneficiary's health, education, support, and maintenance but does not require that any funds be used for those purposes. The age you choose is up to you, and sometimes people will even hold back part of the inheritance until the beneficiary's retirement age, in effect funding a retirement plan for them. Nowadays with fewer employers funding pension plans and the uncertainty of Social Security, this isn't a bad idea. The trustee is in charge of the funds, not the beneficiary. It continues:

When the person for whom the property is held attains the age of 30 years, one-third of the remainder of that person's share of the trust being held for him or her shall thereupon be distributed to him or her free of trust. Upon attaining age 35, one-half the remainder shall be distributed to him or her with the remainder being distributed to him or her upon attaining age 40. If the person should die before attaining the age of 40, the property shall then be paid and distributed to the estate of the person or her trust if any under a power of appointment specifically provided for therein. Beneficiaries may not sell, assign, pledge as collateral, borrow against, or otherwise anticipate their expected inheritance from this trust.

Look at the last sentence of that directive. In any case where a beneficiary does not receive the inheritance in a lump sum, it is important that they not be allowed to sell or assign their future benefits. There are numerous companies in the business of trying to buy someone's expected inheritance for a substantial discount. If you allow this, then the beneficiary is able to thwart your intentions and may end up wasting the inheritance—exactly what you were trying to avoid. Plus, the company that bought it then becomes one of your heirs.

Following is an example allowing funds to be used for higher education, the idea being that the beneficiary, upon graduating from high school, can either go on with her education, which would be paid for by the trust, or wait until a later age to collect the inheritance. This creates a strong incentive to get education or job skills.

If any Beneficiary (including but not limited to a grandchild, if any) is under the age of 25 years when the distribution is to be made, the Trustee shall retain any such property and administer and distribute the same for the benefit of the beneficiary, paying to or for the benefit of such person so much of the income and principal of the retained property from time to time, as the Trustee deems advisable for his or her health, education, support, and maintenance. When the person for whom the property is held attains the age of 18 years or graduates from high school, the trustee may distribute funds on behalf of the beneficiary for educational purposes, including monies for living expenses, so long as the beneficiary is achieving passing grades from an accredited university or trade school. When the person for whom the property is held attains the age of 25 years, the remaining property shall thereupon be distributed to him or her free of trust. If the person should die before attaining the age of 25, the principal remaining shall then be paid and distributed to the children of that person, if any, and if none then to the heirs at law of the grantors.

What if one of the beneficiaries dies before you? Typically, you would direct that the share of that deceased person should instead be given to his or her children and if none then to the other of your named heirs equally. Or you could name another specific person or organization (such as a charity or church) to receive that share.

What if all of the beneficiaries die before you and leave no children? In that case, you need to identify to whom your trust assets should be given.

Leaving something to an organization is one option. If you do this, be sure to include the exact name of the organization and its address. Leaving something to "Cure Cancer" or heart disease of some such generic wording is a bad idea. There are hundreds of charities that purport to be for curing diseases. Not all are legitimate, so be specific as to which organization you mean.

Should you use dollar amounts or percentages? Sometimes things change, especially financial circumstances. That is why I recommend percentages rather than dollar amounts when you are making your distribution plan, unless the amounts are modest.

Here's an example: I had a client named Tom. He was a single man who owned his own home outright and who had about $900,000 in other assets. He had two sisters and a brother but had no children. Tom was also very active in his church and directed that at his death, $300,000 was to go to his church with the balance being divided equally among his siblings. Several years later, he took ill, lost his job, spent down his savings, and mortgaged his house but unfortunately did not change the distribution plan in his trust. At the time of his death, the equity in his house and the remaining liquid assets totaled roughly only $350,000. So after his funeral expenses and final medical bills the entire balance of his estate went to the church with none left for his siblings. Tom's intent was to leave the majority of his assets to the two sisters and brother, not the church; but because of the way his trust was written, the church legally got everything. The sisters and brother, who were my clients, were not happy. Had he instead given the church one-fourth of the assets rather than a specific dollar amount, then he would have had a result more consistent with this wishes.

That's not to say you can't, for example, leave $1,000 to each grandchild for instance. Just remember what you have done and keep you trust distribution in line with your current assets.

Who do you want to make medical decisions for you if you are unable to do so for yourself? Medical directives are very important, and most states even have fill-in-the-blank approved forms available at hospitals and libraries or online. Having a named medical decision maker is crucial if the person you want is not a legal spouse, parent, or child. Your nonrelated partner may have nothing to say about your treatment and in fact may not even be allowed to see you in certain hospital emergency or critical care situations. Note that the medical power of attorney is not the same as the so-called "living will," which states your desires in making end-of-life decisions.

Husband choices	Wife choices
1._____	1._____
2._____	2._____
(Alternate(	
3._____	3._____
(2nd Alternate)	

Do you have an existing trust or will? If so, take a copy to the attorney. He may amend or replace the documents, but having a look at what you have now will be helpful.

Also take the attorney copies of the deeds to all real estate you own as well as the first page of any land contracts.

If you are a member of a prepaid legal plan, please be sure your attorney is a participating member of that plan, since your legal fees may be covered by that plan all or in part.

APPENDIX D

Asset Listing Form

List your assets and approximate values, as this is information needed by the lawyer but is not always easily remembered. It also is very helpful to your trustee so that nothing is left unclaimed. Some people are uncomfortable revealing this to the lawyer, but remember that anything you say or show to the attorney is confidential.

	Your Asset	Spouse's Asset	Joint Asset
Real Estate			
Home	$_____	$_____	$_____
Vacation Home	$_____	$_____	$_____
Other Real Estate	$_____	$_____	$_____
Vehicles			
Cars	$_____	$_____	$_____
Boats	$_____	$_____	$_____
Motor Home	$_____	$_____	$_____
Other Vehicles/ Equipment	$_____	$_____	$_____

Investments			
IRAs	$_____	$_____	$_____
Money Market	$_____	$_____	$_____
Stocks/Bonds	$_____	$_____	$_____
Other Tax Deferred	$_____	$_____	$_____
Pension/Stock Options	$_____	$_____	$_____
Cash Accounts			
Savings	$_____	$_____	$_____
Average Checking	$_____	$_____	$_____
Gold/Precious Metals	$_____	$_____	$_____
Broker Accounts	$_____	$_____	$_____
Insurance			
Life (face amount)	$_____	$_____	$_____
Annuities	$_____	$_____	$_____
Prepaid Burial	$_____	$_____	$_____
Miscellaneous			
Jewelry, Antiques, Collectables	$_____	$_____	$_____
Receivables	$_____	$_____	$_____
Expected Inheritances	$_____	$_____	$_____
Business Interests	$_____	$_____	$_____
Household Goods	$_____	$_____	$_____
Online Accounts	$_____	$_____	$_____
Domain Names, Websites	$_____	$_____	$_____
Patents, Royalties, Copyrights	$_____	$_____	$_____
Other Assets (describe)	$_____	$_____	$_____
TOTALS	$_____	$_____	$_____

APPENDIX E

FAQs

The following are not intended as specific legal advice but illustrate some common concerns we hear from clients and their families.

1. *My aunt died and had a trust, and my brother is the trustee. He won't tell me anything or give me a copy. What can I do?*

Had the trust included specific instructions for the brother as to his legally required duties as trustee, this likely would not have happened. All too often, we see the attitude of the named trustee, the "one in charge," as being secretive. In truth, the trustee's actions are supposed to be totally transparent insofar as the assets of the trust relate to the inheritance left to the particular trust beneficiaries. So while you have no right to decision-making regarding the trust, you certainly should be entitled to a copy of the trust document relating to your inheritance. Typically, someone in your position would submit a written request for copies and an accounting of assets, and if that fails, have an attorney send a similar demand letter. As a last resort, your attorney could ask the local court to intervene and force your brother to comply with the law and even account for all the assets and expenses of the trust.

2. *My parents left a simple instruction in their trust saying that everything be divided equally among the four of us adult children. The problem is not with the money but with the personal stuff, like furniture, family heirlooms, and my dad's gun collection. Some is valuable while others just have sentimental value. Can the trustee just do whatever she wants? She is planning on having an auction.*

One of the problematic areas is personal property. When the heirs cannot agree on how things should be divided, then the auction is a sort of last resort. The problem is that the kids are in a position then of having to bid against strangers for the family things. One way this is solved is with an agreement where the four of you draw straws to see who goes first, second, third, and fourth, and then choose items one at a time in order until everything anyone wants is gone; then you can auction or tag sale the rest. Your parents, as the makers of the trust, could have specified who would get certain specific items in their trust paperwork, which would have eliminated this problem. They also could have specified the procedure to be used to dispose of personal property.

3. *What happens if the trustee who is to take over after the death of the trust maker refuses the job or dies and there is no second choice named?*

Typically, there is a default provision in a trust that states that in the event there is no named successor trustee willing or able to act as trustee, then the beneficiaries, by majority vote, can pick a trustee to administer the estate. If there is no such provision in the trust and no surviving successor trustee, then the courts have the ability to name a trustee to wrap up the estate. If you are forced to petition the court, be sure to request the appointment of one of the beneficiaries as the new trustee so that the court does not appoint an expensive public administrator or attorney to that job. Check with your attorney for local practice and procedure in this case.

4. *My wife and I have a premarital agreement that specifies what happens to our individual assets at our deaths. That was several years ago, and now we want to make a trust to avoid probate but want to do something different than what was agreed before we married. Can we do this?*

Yes. In most cases, if you both agree and there is no fraud or coercion involved, you may nullify a premarital agreement and make a new plan. This can be in the form of a trust-based estate plan and may or may not have to include a postmarital agreement. The terms can be whatever the two of you agree upon.

5. *My mother keeps threatening to disinherit me, but I have a copy of her will, and it says I get an equal share with my brother. Is she bluffing? I don't think she can do it.*

She can do it. Wills can be changed so long as a person is mentally competent. The disinheritance has to be done properly, however. In most states, if she just left your name off the new will, you could go into court and ask for your statutory share for the same amount you would have gotten if there was no will at all, the assumption being that she mistakenly left off the natural object of her affection—one of her children. But if in the will and trust she specifically names you and says no part of her estate is to go to you, then you are disinherited. Be nice to your mother; your copy may mean nothing other than what she intended at that time.

6. *Along that line, can I disinherit my wife? We are separated but not divorced, and I don't want her getting any of my stuff and would rather everything go to our children.*

This is an interesting question that has a surprising answer. In most states, you cannot disinherit a wife with a will, but you can with a trust. If you left her nothing—or not very much—in a will, a wife (and in most cases a husband as well) has what is called a "right of election." This means she can accept what was left to her in the will or elect to take what the state law would have given her if you died intestate—that is without a will. This applies to your separate property since jointly owned assets would go to her automatically anyway. The intestate share varies by state and depends upon whether or not the person who died had children. A quick Internet check can give you the intestate share of a spouse in your state. In the situation you describe, since you have children, your spouse would generally get one-half your assets and the children would get the other half. Or she might get the first $50,000 and half the balance. But again, it depends on state law, and the rules vary. However, this applies only to probated assets. As we know from this book, assets in a trust are not probated; therefore, at least in most states, you can put your assets in a separate trust of your own and leave them to whomever you want and leave none of them to your spouse if you like. I have to repeat, though, that state laws change all the time and are not uniform, so ask your lawyer.

7. *My father was married to my mother for 45 years before she died. Now he has remarried to a woman with her own adult children. My concern is that he, being much older than her, will die first, leaving everything to his wife, then she will leave it all to her children at her death. She and I do not get along, and it seems unfair to have her move in on what should be my inheritance.*

This is a common situation that has both a legal and nonlegal answer. The nonlegal answer is that in a marriage of older people, the couple are usually most concerned with caring for each other. Your father would likely want his assets left to care for his wife before he worries about you. So she would be a natural heir, and laws in most states recognize that and protect her in various ways. The legal answer is first that your father's assets belong to him, not you. You have zero right to any claim whatsoever unless he either dies intestate or leaves you something specifically in his trust or will. There are numerous ways he could provide for you if he choses to do so. For example, he could name you as a beneficiary of a life insurance policy or as a pay-on-death beneficiary of a particular investment or asset account. He could make you a co-owner with right of survivorship on a parcel of real estate. He could create a trust that allows his wife the use of all his assets for her lifetime with the remainder to you at her death. There are many things he could do, but you can't make him do any of them. Wouldn't hurt to let him read this book to give him some ideas.

8. *My mother died and my father is still alive, but he has dementia and lives with me. Dad was married before and had two children by that marriage whom he never sees. Dad has no will, and I am worried that when he dies, my half siblings will show up and want part of his estate. What can I do?*

See a lawyer. Your father cannot now make a will or trust due to his mental incapacity. Unfortunately for you, half siblings share equally if there is no trust or will. There are situations where a person has made a power of attorney that specifically allows an attorney-in-fact to make gifts or even create wills or trusts for a person without it being called self-dealing. And it may be that your father has already provided in his own legal documents for this situation. But you need legal advice to see what your options are. I can't give specific legal advice to anyone via this book since there are so many unknowns and specific circumstances in addition to the complexity and conflict of laws in the various states.

9. *I have no children and am very close to my dogs. I want to set up a plan so that after my death, all my pets are taken care of for their lifetimes.*

All states except Minnesota allow you to create a trust for a pet, whether the pet is a dog, cat, alligator, or whatever. The trust provides a certain amount of money to be set aside in an account for the pets with a trustee who carries out the distribution of the money to the caregiver, who is often also the trustee. You may specify the kind of care you want given, including the type of food, exercise, medical treatment, grooming—anything. It's important to specify the pets by name and have implanted microchips, or you can just say any pets you own at the time of your death. There should be a remainder-man—that is, the person or organization that gets any funds left over after the animals die. You may specify a sum to be paid to the caregiver for acting as such, either a set amount or an annual amount. These trusts typically can last no more than twenty-one years, but state laws vary.

As an aside, there is the story of a person who set up a trust for her cat, leaving a large annual payment to the caregiver for the lifetime of the cat. The bank trustee would visit annually to check on the pet's welfare. After thirty-two years, the bank became suspicious and eventually discovered the caregiver had substituted a new identically looking cat when the first one died, then again when the second died. The annual payments stopped.

10. *We own a summer cottage and have taken our four children there many times over their lifetimes. We would like to keep the cottage in the family for use by them and their children and even their grandchildren. Can we do this with a trust?*

Yes, but it is not necessarily a good idea. I hear this frequently, but I also hear from the next generation down who wish their parents had never set the cottage up that way. There are many issues that occur after your deaths. The children often move away from the area where they grew up and have their own families. It may be that the cottage is many hundreds or thousands of miles from where they end up, and so they use the cottage little or not at all. Often there is one family that uses the cottage a lot and others not so much. But it is in a sense jointly owned, so the joint assets in the trust that take care of the property are benefitting some of the children but not all. If no fund were set up to cover things like taxes, insurance, utilities, and maintenance, all of the children would be responsible for paying those expenses, even though they may not get any benefit from those expenses. But if it is set up in a trust, it may be difficult to do anything differently. Then at the death of one of your children, their children may have little or no interest in the cottage or may be minors with no way to pay for the expenses. People have this romantic idea of carrying on what was a wonderful experience for them, but that rarely works smoothly.

But yes, it can be done. To make it work, you would need to answer all the "what if" questions you can think of. What if one of the children wants to opt out? Would they get anything for their share? And if so, from where would the money come? What if one of them refused to pay their share? Do the others have the right to foreclose their interest or make them pay somehow? If one of them dies, does their spouse have the rights to the cottage for his or her lifetime? Can a child sell his or her share to a nonrelated person or borrow against it? Is there money available to set up a permanent fund for cottage expenses? Who decides how to spend that fund? How many generations would this arrangement go on? State laws often limit the length of a trust of this kind. So as you can see, I advise against it. You should consider leaving the cottage to the four children equally and let them figure it out, which is a better plan than tying it up in trust. My opinion, of course.

11. *We have minor children and want to decide who would be their guardian in the event of our deaths. We have someone in mind. Can this be done with a trust?*

It is possible to do it with a trust, but a better practice is to include those wishes in your pour-over will. As discussed earlier in this volume, we always make a pour-over will as a fail-safe mechanism to direct assets that were left out of the trust to pour into the trust to be distributed in the same manner as the other trust assets. Wills have to be probated if they meet the state dollar amount threshold for probate; in most cases, the trust is fully funded, so there are no assets to probate by will. However, the directives as to guardianship of minors that are contained in the will would be used by the court to set up the guardianship and conservatorship for those children. So while the will would not be probated, it would still be used for the guardian appointment.

Glossary of Terms

beneficiary: In a trust, the person who benefits from the trust assets. Initially, the beneficiary will be the grantor, then at the death of the grantor, the beneficiaries are the people or organizations named in the trust who are to receive the trust assets. *Heir* is sometimes used to mean beneficiary.

conservator: A person appointed by a court to be the financial manager of the assets of a minor or an incapacitated or incompetent adult.

Employer Identification Number: A number issued by the IRS to use as the taxpayer number for the trust. This is like a Social Security Number for a person.

estate and inheritance taxes: Taxes paid to the state or federal government based upon a percentage of the total taxable estate of a deceased person. Typically, no taxes are due unless the total estate size exceeds a preset threshold amount.

fiduciary: A person who is in a special position of trust regarding the financial affairs of another.

funding: The process of transferring assets to a trust.

grantor: The person who creates the trust is the grantor. Also sometimes called the *settlor* or *trustor*.

guardian: A person appointed by a court to care for a minor or a legally disabled adult. The guardian cares for the person while the conservator cares for the person's financial affairs.

heir: A person who inherits property from a person who dies, whether through a will, a trust, or a beneficiary designation. Also commonly called a *beneficiary*.

intestate: A person who dies without a will is said to have died intestate, whereas one who dies with a will is said to have died testate. Think last will and *testament*.

issue: The direct blood-related descendants of a person, i.e., children, grandchildren, great grandchildren.

joint tenancy: A co-ownership of property by two or more parties in which each party owns an undivided interest that passes to the other co-owner on her death (known as the "right of survivorship").

life tenant: A person who has the right to the use of certain property for his lifetime. For real estate, this right is sometimes called a life lease or a life estate.

living trust: A written document that, when signed and funded properly, becomes a legal entity that has the ability to control the assets it owns and states who will receive those assets under certain conditions as well as who is in charge of seeing that these instructions are carried out. (Simply, who gets what, when they get it, and who is in charge of seeing that that happens.)

patient advocate: The person who acts under a medical power of attorney to make medical decisions for a person who is unable to make those decisions for herself. This is done by appointment in a medical power of attorney.

personal representative: This is the person who is in charge of the probate of an estate. Sometimes called an executor where there is a will, or an administrator where there is no will.

power of attorney: A document that gives a person (an agent, sometimes called an attorney-in-fact) the legal right to transact the business of another person (the principal). This permission to sign is limited to the exact rights set out in the document as though the original principal had signed himself. Sometimes called a proxy. A durable power of attorney is one that is still valid even if the principal becomes incapacitated. A springing power of attorney is one that becomes effective only upon the happening of a certain event, such as a person becoming incapacitated (a person could have a springing durable power of attorney). A power of attorney is valid until it is revoked or the principal dies.

probate: A legal court process through which assets in the name of the deceased person are transferred to those who are entitled to them after paying all debts of the deceased and the expenses of administering the probate case. Probate may be used to settle disputes as to the validity of a will, trust, or other document. The probate court has authority over all issues relating to the financial affairs of deceased persons. Separate sections of the probate court may involve the affairs of minors, juvenile offenses, guardianships, conservatorships, and handicapped adults.

revocable living trust: A living trust in which terms may be amended, modified, or otherwise revoked by the grantor during her lifetime, as opposed to an irrevocable trust, which may not be changed once created. A revocable trust typically becomes an irrevocable trust at the death or incapacity of the grantor.

rule against perpetuities: A state law determining how long a trust may stay in existence.

special-needs trust: A trust that manages assets for a beneficiary who may be unable to manage his own financial affairs, typically to pay for living expenses beyond those provided by agencies and programs such as Medicaid and set things up so that the beneficiary is not disqualified from those aid plans.

successor trustee: The person who is in charge of the trust assets at the death or incapacity of the grantor. If the grantor is incapacitated mentally or physically so as to be unable to manage the trust, the successor trustee manages the grantor's business affairs during that time.

At the grantor's death, the successor trustee is responsible for carrying out the grantor's instructions as written in the trust for the distribution of the trust assets, as well as taking care of any tax issues for the estate.

tenants in common: Where two or more people own property jointly but each has separate ownership of her share without a right of survivorship with the other co-owners. A tenant in common may transfer her separate share of an asset without the permission of the other owners in most cases.

testator: A person who makes a will. If the person is female, a testatrix. Archaic language.

trustee: The person who is in charge of the trust assets and who carries out the instructions in the trust. Normally the grantor is the trustee during his lifetime. At the grantor's death or incapacity, the successor trustee takes over.

trust protector: A person (or group of people) appointed in a trust document to oversee the trustee. This person sometimes has the power to modify the terms of the trust herself.

Index

A

A/B trusts, 44, 83, 105, 111
ancillary probate, 29
arbitration, 31
asset location at death, 114–117
asset protection, 88
attorneys
  fees, viii, x, xiv, 2–4, 8, 25, 30, 31, 37–46, 52, 86, 93, 97, 154
  finding one, 45–49
  the attorney annual review, 50

B

beneficiaries, ix, 7, 8, 13–18, 22, 29, 41, 44, 52–59, 61–69, 71–76, 80–88, 104–116, 123, 144, 150–152, 158, 161
blended families, 18, 53, 62, 66, 107

C

children, 11, 16–19, 22, 23, 38, 42-52, 62, 66, 74, 77, 80, 125
conservators, ix, 2, 11–13, 22–24, 58, 59, 92–96, 104
creditors, 3, 27, 28, 76, 78, 88, 89, 103, 118, 119, 127, 129

D

death or disability of trust maker, 101–125

deeds, 5, 6, 29, 44, 51, 62, 63, 70,76, 77, 104
descent and distribution, 6
disabled beneficiaries, ix, x, 14, 15, 22, 23, 51, 56, 58, 80, 95, 101, 124, 125
divorce, 71, 72

E
education trusts, 55, 72, 81, 84
estate taxes, ix, 8, 9, 20, 21, 33, 44, 45, 80–84, 89, 105, 111, 117

F
family and marital trusts, 83, 84, 111
FAQs
Appendix E, 157
fiduciaries, 8, 54, 103, 165
funding of trusts
methods, 61–63
vehicles, boats, aircraft, 65, 66
personal property, 66
real estate, 66
insurance and annuities, 62
stocks, investment accounts, 75
bank/credit union accounts, 64
tax deferred/retirement accounts, 75, 76
other assets, 67

G
gay couples, 17, 82
guardians
for adults, 22, 24, 57, 58, 92–96, 102
for children, ix, 11, 12, 57, 89–92

I
individual trusts, 19, 71, 82, 83
inheritance taxes, 105 (*See also* estate taxes)
instructions at death or disability, 101–125
intestacy, 6, 42,43, 160

J
joint ownership of assets, 5, 22, 62, 68, 74–76
joint trusts, 20, 21, 55, 71, 82
unmarried couples, 17
gay couples, 17, 82
other joint trusts, 17

L
ladybird deed, 77, 78
living wills, 44, 78, 98, 154

N
no-contest clause in trust document, 30

P
pay-on-death designations, 7, 64, 69, 73, 115, 144

personal property
funding into trust, 66
specific gifts to individuals, 66, 98, 104, 117, 158
pet trusts, 67, 161
power of attorney, 24, 74, 78, 93, 95, 167
prepaid legal plans, 35, 154
privacy aspect of trusts, 31
probate, 1–4, 22, 25, 27–30
professional trustees. *See* trustees
prudent investor, 54, 124
publication of death notice, 5, 27, 28, 66, 84, 129

Q

quitclaim deed. *See* deeds

R

real estate, 4, 6, 20, 28, 29, 51, 54–59, 62–76, 94, 98, 104, 113, 117, 123, 125, 143, 154
revoking the trust, 70, 71
royalties, 66, 67

S

separate trusts for couples, 20
separation, divorce, remarriage, 19, 20, 71
small estates, 21, 22
Social Security survivor benefits, 105
special-needs trust , 14, 15, 57, 58, 72, 167
spendthrift trust, 15
successor trustees, 44, 57, 108
instructions on death or disability, 102–125

T

trusts
contesting a trust, 31, 43
continuing trusts, 123–125
certificate of trust, 98, 99
changing the trust, 107
children trusts, 11, 16–19, 22, 23, 38, 42–52, 62, 66, 74, 77, 80, 125
cost, 25, 26, 43
defined, 6–9
education trusts, 55, 72, 81, 84
naming your trust, 7
problems with trusts, 85
settling the trust, 8, 26, 27, 30, 102–104
trust sales companies, 36–38
trust seminars, 33–35
testamentary trust, 9
types of trusts, 79–84
who needs a trust, 11–24
who does not need a trust, 73–78

trustees
children as trustees, 53, 55, 57, 59
cotrustees, 53, 56, 59
defined, 8, 53, 55, 58
powers of trustees, 8, 13, 14, 24, 54, 101
removal of a trustee, 85, 86
successor trustees, 44, 57, 108
spouse as trustee, 55, 59
trustee fees, 44, 56
professional trustees, 55, 56
trust companies and banks, 46, 55, 56, 86
trust protector, 87, 88

U

Uniform Trust Act, 28

W

wills, ix, x, xv, 1–8, 42, 50
pour-over wills, 44, 52, 70, 92, 115, 164

Estate Planning for the Healthy, Wealthy Family
by Carla Garrity, Mitchell Baris, and Stanley Neeleman (6 x 9, 256 pages, ebook, $22.99)

Feng Shui and Money
by Eric Shaffert (6 x 9, 256 pages, paperback, $16.95)

How to Plan and Settle Estates
by Edmund Fleming (6 x 9, 288 pages, paperback, $16.95)

Legal Forms for Everyone, Sixth Edition
by Carl W. Battle (8 ½ x 11, 280 pages, paperback, $24.99)

Legal Guide to Social Media
by Kimberly A. Houser (6 x 9, 208 pages, paperback, $19.95)

Love & Money
by Ann-Margaret Carrozza, Esq. (6 x 9, 248 pages, hardcover, $24.99)

The Money Mentor
by Tad Crawford (6 x 9, 272 pages, paperback, $24.95)

Protecing Your Assets from Probate and Long-Term Care
by Evan H. Farr (6 x 9, 208 pages, paperback, $14.99)

Scammed
by Gini Graham Scott, PhD (6 x 9, 256 pages, paperback, $14.99)

The Secret Life of Money
by Tad Crawford (5 ½ x 8 ½, 304 pages, paperback, $19.95)

The Smart Consumer's Guide to Good Credit
by John Ulzheimer (5 ¼ x 8 ¼, 216 pages, paperback, $14.95)

Your Living Trust & Estate Plan, Fifth Edition
by Harvey J. Platt (6 x 9, 352 pages, paperback, $16.95)

To see our complete catalog or to order online, please visit *www.allworth.com.*